MELTDOWN

MELTDOWN

HOW TO TURN YOUR
HARDSHIP INTO HAPPINESS

JAMIE ALDERTON

RETHINK PRESS

First published in Great Britain in 2019
by Rethink Press (www.rethinkpress.com)

CONTENTS

INTRODUCTION

Life is like a gripping book. A book usually starts off slowly, then something happens in the middle that makes it interesting, and you finally discover how it all ends in the last few chapters. You only get to the final chapters in life when you're on your deathbed and about to take your final breath. Regardless of the struggles you're currently going through, there's always another page to turn and if you persist with it, the chapters start to get better.

> *'Life is so ironic, it takes sadness to know what happiness is, noise to appreciate silence and absence to value presence.'*
>
> BOB CURIANO, songwriter

Back in 2016, I naïvely thought I was flying high in the chapters of my life. Everything was going well for me and I thought that would be how the story ended. Little did I know that I was just getting started, and I was still in the first few chapters of my life.

This book will take you through my 'chapters'. I realise now that I'm not sure how far I am through my chapters because I hope I have a lot of life left to live. What I do know, following my own experience, is that you can take control of the story. I want to show you in this book how you can recover from complete meltdown and make it out on the other side.

We'll explore habits and discover how to understand yourself better. It's important to note that everything you do can be assessed on where it lies between two extremes on a continuous scale. Too much in either direction is bad for your physical and mental health; the key to success is keeping the balance.

I'm going to show you a range of different tools, mental models and practices to help you get the most out of every day and live a healthier, happier and stronger life. To get the greatest benefit from this book, I want you to allocate a time in the day when you can read just one chapter – this is non-negotiable. I don't want you to read more than one chapter a day – even if (and hoping) you can't wait to read the next one!

My aim is for you to complete the book and to grasp fully what I'm teaching in the following chapters, so here is what I want you to do:

> Read – Read one chapter of the book

No more, no less. It's difficult to commit to finishing a book, but pretty easy to commit to reading one chapter a day. I'll explain more about this later on in the book.

> Reflect – Reflect on the points that resonated with you

Reflection is so important. When we wake up in the morning it's as if we're on autopilot, ticking off boxes and getting things done. Once you've finished your chapter, set a timer for three minutes and really think about what you've just read. Consider the stories and ask yourself whether similar things have happened in your own life. Just take this time to examine your thoughts.

> Write – Write down your reflections in your journal or notepad

To truly understand each chapter of this book you need to get your thoughts out of your head and onto paper. We have 40,000–60,000 thoughts every single day, but the only ones that we remember are the ones we write down.

> **Teach – Teach others on social media what you've learned**
> ... And don't forget to tag me in on Instagram: @jayalderton!
>
> When you teach someone else what you've learned you gain a better understanding of it. This also supplies you with content for the day: if you're active on social media and constantly stuck for ideas, this is the perfect plan of action to bring value to your audience.

Before we get to the first chapter, I want to give you a virtual high five. You're already one of the few individuals who are taking control of their lives through reading, and in doing this you're already placing yourself ahead of the crowd. According to government research, 31% of adults in England don't read in their free time, rising to 46% of young people (aged 16–24).[1] This costs the UK £81 billion a year in lost earnings and increased welfare spending – that's a lot of money!

The reason I highlight these statistics is because reading and listening have literally changed my life. I went from being an uneducated, 'un-empathetic' soldier

---

1 The Department for Digital, Culture, Media & Sport: https://readingagency. org.uk/about/impact/002-reading-facts-1/#fn10

with barely any academic qualifications ten years ago to becoming a bestselling author, entrepreneur and coach, transforming the lives of thousands through my books, blogs and videos. I'm proud of this, but make no mistake: I'm nothing special. Anyone can do it if they're willing to be disciplined, avoid distractions and use the abundance of free resources out there on the internet.

Let this book help you to become more productive, to get out of any 'funk' you are currently in, and to reach the levels of success you deserve.

I'll see you on the other side, folks.

Jamie

BREAKING DOWN AND BREAKING THROUGH

The year 2016 was one of my most successful in business and personal development. I was ticking all the boxes and achieving everything that I set out to do. I felt invincible, having just opened my dream gym facility at the same time as writing a bestselling book. It had been a crazy year full of excitement and uncertainty. I knew starting a new business was going to take my full, undivided attention if it was to do well. I would need to get to my gym before anyone else and finish later than anyone else to set the pace for my new employees.

We had organised to do a charity event in October, with eight of the team pushing a sled for twenty-four hours to raise money for a local hospice that cared for my grandad before he passed away. As the day got nearer, I had this mad idea of doing the entire event myself. Sure enough, when I told the team I would be doing it on my own they thought I was crazy.

But with six weeks of training and twenty-four hours of grit and determination, I set a new world record by pushing a 140kg sled over 16 miles, raising £10,000 for charity in the process. This opened up a new way of thinking for me, and I was astounded at just how much you can put your body through if your mind is strong. Little did I know that this was just the start of the journey.

GOING IT ALONE

My business was really taking off, and the week after the event I launched my first book, *Mindset with Muscle*,[2] which I had been working on throughout the year as I was building up the gym. To my complete surprise, the book became one of the fastest bestsellers on Amazon and hit the number one spot in just eight hours! To top it all off, I then discovered my podcast had hit the number one spot on iTunes.

I remember waking up the morning after feeling like I was walking on a cloud – what a year it had been. Then... something came over me. It felt like I had fallen off the cloud and had a deep void in my life, as if I'd been forgetting something.

---

2 J Alderton (2016) *Mindset With Muscle: Proven strategies to build up your brain, body and business.* Gorleston: Rethink Press.

It was now December. Six months had passed since I started working on my dreams and opened my new business. I'm very reflective at this time of year, as I look back to all the things I set out to do at the start of the year and assess what was successful and what was not. It hit me that I had totally forgotten about my reasons for doing all these things in the first place. It was for my wife Anna and my daughter Elyza.

A huge guilt descended on me as I slowly came to realise that all this achievement was focused on myself. I hadn't shared any of this success with the people I love, and I hadn't really brought them into my goals and dreams as a family. Some disturbing thoughts began to run through my mind. 'Do I even need them anymore? I mean, 2016 was incredible but it's just the start of big things and now I'm afraid they will be holding me back.' But I also thought to myself, 'Stop having these thoughts, Jamie. They are so egotistical it's unreal!'

My head was all over the place and I started to deal with these issues the best way I knew: with alcohol. The week after the book launch and charity event I was drinking a bottle of wine, and sometimes two, on my own every single night. For over a month I became a 'functioning alcoholic', and whenever my wife and daughter went out, I would head to the shop, grab a bottle of wine and ease the pain of the thoughts going through my head.

It was easy to convince myself that I didn't have a problem. I'd sit and drink while I wrote blogs and content, and this was how I justified what I was doing. 'I'm more creative when I'm a little drunk,' I'd say to myself, which was a poor excuse.

One Friday, Anna and Elyza had gone out. Anna and I were supposed to be sharing a bottle of wine once they got back. When Anna came in, she noticed that I had almost finished a bottle by myself and we got into an argument about this. It was at that moment, in my drunken state, that I said to Anna, 'I'm out!'

'What do you mean "I'm out"?' she asked.

'I'm out of this relationship; I don't love you any more,' I said.

We spent two hours crying and shouting at each other, with me saying, 'I no longer feel anything,' then leaving the house and walking the seven miles to my 'dream gym facility'. I had a photoshoot there in the morning alongside all of my gym members, so I decided to sleep on my office floor that night.

Looking back at this time, I realise that Anna saw what was going on in my head and she refused to accept the things I was saying. I have been with Anna since the age of thirteen and there is no one on the planet who knows me better. I sometimes think she knows me better than I know myself.

We had some deep and meaningful conversations over the Christmas period and we both decided that in order for me to truly understand what was going on I needed to move out. In January I rented a flat near my gym facility for six months. I was excited to finally have my own 'lad pad': a place where I could be on my own with my thoughts and feelings.

This was difficult to deal with from a social media point of view. I was going through one of the darkest times in my life, yet I had to show up every day and pretend that everything was fine so I could carry on with the business. People would ask me if I had moved out and say, 'what's with the new flat?' and I would respond with, 'It's my new place to chill, read and get creative.'

I spent thousands on this flat, buying everything you could imagine: brand-new sofas, a flat-screen TV and the sort of furniture I had always wanted. For some strange reason, I thought that this would make me happy, and I was pleased about my decision to move out and set up on my own.

But you know what I felt? I felt isolated, lonely and miserable. I spent hardly any time in the flat. I went there only to drown my sorrows and shut myself away from what was going on around me.

Again, I was doing what I knew worked best... drinking my two bottles of red wine each night before going to sleep. I remember a few nights when I woke up on the sofa or on the floor of the flat, with wine all over me, having drunk myself to sleep. I had never felt so lonely and I realised that I was going deeper and deeper into a very dark place. This was not what I had imagined and it was a million miles away from the life that I truly wanted.

The flat was a stupid and expensive decision – I realised that as soon as I moved in. I was taking a decent salary as director of my company, but even that wouldn't cover the two grand a month I needed to cover all the expenses of my new living arrangements.

THE CHALLENGE OF CHANGE

I decided with a friend that we'd run a thirty-day challenge, in which we'd hold people accountable for their habits and actions. We had over 300 people participating, which allowed me to clear the debt I had on the flat.

Despite my troubles, one thing I'd always been good at was business and solving problems – even though I was struggling to solve the biggest problem I had ever had. But running this accountability challenge made me realise where I had been going wrong in the past year.

The challenge meant that each day you had to review your accountability across four categories and rate it on a scale of 1 to 5. The four categories were:

> Health – How healthy have your levels of exercise and nutrition been today?

> Wealth – How have you improved your wealth today?

> Productivity – How productive have you been today?

> Connectivity – How many real (as opposed to virtual) people have you connected with today?

I look at each of these categories as legs on a stool. It doesn't matter how strong three of these legs are, if the fourth one is not solid, the stool would become unstable.

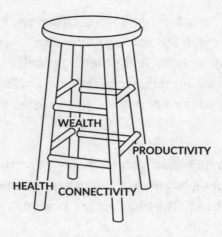

For thirty days I did the challenge along with the other entrants and this was how my days worked out:

> Health – Despite the drinking, I was eating healthily and being very active, so 3 out of 5

> Wealth – The business was growing, so most days would score 4 out of 5

> Productivity – I had been incredibly productive in January, so usually 4 out of 5

> Connectivity – Ah... yes... Well... OK, so maybe 1 or 2 on a good day

It took the month of January and a thirty-day challenge to make me realise this was not the life I wanted to live.

It dawned on me that I was being incredibly selfless with my time to complete strangers, but not allocating any of my time to those that I really cared about.

I had gone from being an incredibly selfish person over the past three years as a competitor, focused only on my own training and physique, to being an incredibly selfless person as a coach. The balance needed to be restored and I had to have time to figure this out on my own.

It was at this point that I found an Airbnb in Spain and decided to isolate myself for three days, alone and away from social media. It was time to ignore everyone's emails, messages and requests and delve deep into how I was going to get out of the 'meltdown' I was having.

If you're going through a tough time at the moment, I want to let you know that everything will be fine. These events are here to build us, not break us. In the following chapters I'm going to show you exactly how I used this period of withdrawal to build happiness, sharing with you the tricks and tools that I used to get out of the funk that I was in and flip everything around to improve my relationship with myself and the people I love.

TASK

My 'Meltdown Management Scale' is all about identifying what you need to work on.

The scale measures four simple aspects of your daily life, as in the challenge above: health, wealth, productivity and connectivity. I will ask you at the end of each chapter to give yourself a mark between 1 and 5 for each element. As we go along, I'll be giving you tools and strategies so you can improve in each area and achieve higher scores as we progress.

But before you start marking yourself later in this chapter (which will give you your baseline mark), I want to describe how to assess each of the elements and set out the marking scheme.

HEALTH

Health goes beyond having a six-pack and low levels of body fat. Health is being happy and confident in your own skin, both physically and mentally. Please take the time to look at both of these aspects and ask yourself whether you're exercising each week, improving your strength – and whether you can look in the mirror and say to yourself honestly that you're in a good place in both the physical and mental aspects of your life.

WEALTH

Wealth goes beyond how much money you have in the bank. For this measurement I want you to assess your income, but also your job satisfaction. Do you have a roof over your head and know where your next meal is coming from? Have a look at your social wealth too: do you have family and friends around you each day? Delve 'deeper than the dollar' on this one.

PRODUCTIVITY

Are you ticking boxes each day and pushing the needle forward? Succeeding is great, but without appropriate measurement, it can come at a cost, which is why I want you to look at the scale of your productivity. Are you learning to say no to people and delegating the things you don't enjoy doing to others? We will be looking at how you can improve your productivity in more detail in the coming chapters, but for now be as honest as you can about where you stand with this.

CONNECTIVITY

With connectivity, we are looking at both your physical and emotional connection with people. Connecting with friends and family on social media is *not* connectivity. Depending on your work and family circumstances, you may, as I do, have regular physical contact with people, but connecting emotionally is vitally important too, so make sure that you are assessing yourself correctly in the early chapters.

THE MELTDOWN MANAGEMENT SCALE

The marking scheme for the assessments is set out in the table below.

Chapter 1 scoring	
Health (mental and physical)	
1 – Poor and in desperate need of improvement	
2 – Below average	
3 – Average	
4 – Above average	
5 – Elite	
Wealth (financial and social)	
1 – Struggling with finances and in desperate need of improvement	
2 – Below average	
3 – Average	
4 – Above average	
5 – An abundance of financial and social wealth	
Productivity	
1 – Struggling to get even the smallest task completed each day	
2 – Below average	
3 – Average	
4 – Above average	
5 – A productivity machine	
Connectivity (physical and emotional)	
1 – Barely connect with anyone physically on a daily basis	
2 – Connect with people physically once a week	
3 – Connect with people physically 2–3 times a week	
4 – Connect with people physically and emotionally 3–5 times a week	
5 – Connect with people physically and emotionally every day	
Total	
Average	

PHONE SWAP THURSDAYS

Back to January 2017 and I had just booked my flight to Spain and told everyone on my social media that I'd not be available for three days (the longest I'd ever been off social media).

When I got to the airport it felt strange not checking my phone for likes and comments. Instant boredom came over me and I started to look on my phone for apps that don't involve connecting with people on social media. (At the time I still had my phone but to stop me using Twitter, Facebook, Instagram and Snapchat, I deleted them.)

I remembered downloading an app called Medium, which was a blogging site, and I allowed myself to use this app as it was in the rules that I had set for myself on this three-day challenge.

Medium is social in its own way. You go there to consume blogs and articles from smart people. It's different from Facebook and Instagram where you might follow a friend or a colleague and get caught up in what they're doing or complaining about. It made me realise that we spend hours consuming pointless content on social media that doesn't help us get healthier, happier, fitter and stronger.

After an hour on Medium, I felt creative, enlightened and motivated to get out my notepad and jot down some new ideas. It had been a long time since I had done this, and it brought me way back to my first taste of self-development when I discovered it in 2013. Back then, social media was different. It was a lot more sociable and most people I knew used it to connect with others and make friends. I read and absorbed so much then, mainly from physical books and podcasts which were just on the rise. The knowledge I gained in that period became the turning point in my life; it changed my thinking and grew my mind.

Today, I don't consume half as much as I used to, as social media is now my full-time job. I'm very much a creator, writing blogs and making podcasts, so much so that I sometimes forget to take the time to consume them myself.

Looking back at my life over the past three years, I have been pretty much 'on' with my business and social media. I'm super consistent with posting content and responding to my audience, and thanks to this I've managed to grow a successful business.

There's just one thing I didn't think about: how it would look to other people. Most of my family and friends don't really know what I do for a living and they watch me spend hours on my mobile phone talking and typing. If they told me to put it down, I would rudely tell them that my entire business is run on it and I've got hundreds of messages every single day that I need to respond to. It's pretty awesome carrying your business in your pocket and delivering a service to customers and clients. If ever they need me, I'm back to them in less than thirty minutes – how great is that?

It wasn't until I was unavailable for three solid days that I realised this was the issue.

DISCIPLINE

Having three days away without any distractions made me see how much of a distraction social media can be. Without set rules in place, you can literally waste hours each day which could be better used either pushing the needle forward in your business or 'wasting that time well' with the people you love.

During the building of my gym facility, my wife and I went to Sorrento, Italy, which to me is one of the most beautiful places in the world. I was walking along a beach with golden sands and wooden huts; it was so peaceful. Then I saw a sign that said 'Free Wi-Fi' and immediately got my phone out to connect to it.

Big mistake.

I was suddenly inundated with hundreds of notifications, messages, tags and pictures, which I couldn't actually see because the wi-fi was so bad. I immediately forgot where I was and got caught up in the blurry images and buffering texts on my mobile phone. Goodbye stress-free Italy and hello stress-full work.

Being available all the time is great for your customers and clients but pretty much sucks for you. The amazing thing about a 'brick-and-mortar' business is that you can close its doors at the end of the day. Sure, you don't have your business in your pocket and you don't make any sales after hours, but at least you can switch off from time to time.

Running both a physical and online business meant that I was 'open all hours' and would feel guilty if I didn't respond to people right away. My clients would expect it from me, which is why they pay me, right?

Well, not really...

If you answer your customers' and clients' messages late at night they will think they can message you at any time, and when you don't respond they will most likely be annoyed.

If your clients or customers message you and they get an auto-response saying that all messages are answered between 9am and 4pm, they will most likely wait until the morning for it to be solved. I'm an online coach and trainer, so any question my clients have at 10pm can wait until the morning to be answered.

Discipline is incredibly important when running an online business, as is having set rules in place for yourself as well as your customers and clients. Your response to your customers', clients' and followers' messages can't be deleted; they are permanent. Have you ever emailed a shitty response to a person only to regret it as soon as you've sent it? Ever argued online with someone at midnight after one too many gins? I certainly have, and I bet you have too.

Your discipline is like a battery: when you wake up in the morning it is fully charged. Everything you see and do throughout the day drains your battery and, depending on the day, your discipline is depleted at different speeds. Once the battery is dead, the worst thing you can do is respond to messages and emails, let alone respond to others online who might have got a little upset with you.

Look at your discipline like a mobile phone. When we have all the apps running and we're constantly on it, it doesn't take long for its battery to drain. If we're constantly fighting fires and responding to people all day, it's not long before our discipline battery is drained too.

If you want the battery on your phone to last all day, you can turn off Bluetooth, reduce the brightness of the screen and turn off wi-fi.

If you want your discipline battery to last all day, you can turn off social media at 8pm, remove negative and draining people from your life and swap your mobile phone on Thursdays.

THE PRINCIPLE OF POLARITY

My three-day trip to Spain was life-changing. For three solid days I was in my head and my books, writing notes and coming up with lots of ideas. I had so many realisations out there that when I came back, I knew what I had to do.

A long time ago, I read a book on hermetic philosophy called *The Kybalion*.[3] It was a pretty 'out there' book but I remember one of the principles that stuck with me, the 'Principle of Polarity':

> *'Everything is Dual; everything has poles; everything has its pair of opposites; like and unlike are the same; opposites are identical in nature, but different in degree; extremes meet; all truths are but half-truths; all paradoxes may be reconciled.'*

What I discovered is that there are two extremes on the same scale. The scale that I am measuring is Selfishness and Unselfishness and their relationships with each other.

When you become extremely selfish, you can prioritise your own needs over those of others and become more

---

3 Three Initiates (2018) *The Kybalion: Hermetic philosophy.* New York: Random House.

productive and successful. Athletes and bodybuilders have to be extremely selfish if they want to succeed in becoming world class at what they are doing. No one is going to run the laps or lift the weights for you – this is something you must do by yourself.

Extreme selfishness has huge downsides though, as it makes you look a bit of an asshole, not caring about others as much as yourself. If you put the needs of others before yourself, people value you more. Opportunities arise with being extremely selfless, as to others you become reliable, consistent and a go-to person for problem-solving.

Mothers are extremely selfless with their children and will always put their children's needs first. When you're a baby you can't do anything yourself and the only way you can communicate with others is to cry and moan until the problem is solved. Sadly, I see that a lot of grown-ups still live like this, but we'll leave that thought for another book.

Being extremely selfless has its downsides too. If you put everyone's needs before your own, you forget to care for the most important person in your life... you. If your health and mindset are fucked, how can you help make others better?

You can't pour from an empty cup. Or as Eleanor Brownn said, 'you can't serve from an empty vessel'. Suddenly the whole principle of polarity started to make sense. In my bodybuilding days I was an extremely selfish person, achieving British and European titles because I always put myself before others.

Nowadays, at least in the past year, I put the needs of others before myself. Sure, I benefitted from these needs, gaining clients and business, but it was an eighteen-hour day, seven-days-a-week schedule which didn't allow me to fill up my own cup. I had been pouring from an empty cup for far too long and in a few short years I had risen up the polarity scale from extreme selfishness to extreme selflessness, but this selflessness was focused on complete strangers and not on the people who needed it most – my family and friends.

The answer to solving this was in ancient Greek philosophy: I must concentrate upon the opposite and go back to my old ways of extreme selfishness for a little while so that I could even out the scale and sort my shit out. My Yes will now become a No. If you email me, there is a strong chance I won't get back to you. If you message me, I probably won't respond, and if you need me to do something for you, I will probably be too busy.

This is where the concept of Phone Swap Thursdays has come from. Every Thursday I now swap my phone for a cheap, old phone that has zero social media on it and the only thing I can do on it is make calls and send texts. This day feels strange, because I'm so used to going into my pocket and using my phone, but since doing this I have managed to connect with people better and get so much more done on this day.

I want to challenge you to do the same. Make Thursdays your selfish day and swap your mobile phone. You can pick spare phones up for less than twenty pounds now on Amazon or eBay or, better yet, just go without a phone completely on this day. Spend this time doing selfish things, which can also be selfless too. Go and do something fun with people, go to a coffee shop with a good book and get lost in it, drive to a forest or park and go exploring. Do things that make you forget you have an Instagram account.

TASK

I've created the Selfishness Scale as a measurement for you to be honest with yourself and ask if you're doing too much for others or too much for yourself. The main focus of the scale is for you to focus on the right things for your phone swap Thursdays. If you are doing too much for yourself, your Thursdays need to be focused on connecting with others. If your scale is doing too much for others, you need to focus your Thursdays on connecting with yourself.

Doing too much for others	Extreme selflessness
Become uncontactable	Say yes to everything
Put your needs first	Prioritise others' needs first
Look after yourself	Put others' needs first
Say no to everything	Proactively reach out to others
Extreme selfishness	Doing too much for yourself

The Selfishness Scale

Ready for your first Phone Swap Thursday? Next, you need to do your Meltdown Management Scale and mark each one from 1 to 5.

Chapter 2 scoring	
Health (mental and physical)	
1 – Poor and in desperate need of improvement	
2 – Below average	
3 – Average	
4 – Above average	
5 – Elite	
Wealth (financial and social)	
1 – Struggling with finances and in desperate need of improvement	
2 – Below average	
3 – Average	
4 – Above average	
5 – An abundance of financial and social wealth	
Productivity	
1 – Struggling to get even the smallest task completed each day	
2 – Below average	
3 – Average	
4 – Above average	
5 – A productivity machine	
Connectivity (physical and emotional)	
1 – Barely connect with anyone physically on a daily basis	
2 – Connect with people physically once a week	
3 – Connect with people physically 2–3 times a week	
4 – Connect with people physically and emotionally 3–5 times a week	
5 – Connect with people physically and emotionally every day	
Total	
Average	

RUNNING AVERAGES

Ch. 1	Ch. 2

CHAPTER 3

FINDING STOICISM

During my journey through my meltdown, I found that a lot of businesspeople and entrepreneurs talk about stoicism. If you were to meet me in person you would find that I am naturally stoic. I internalise a lot of things and when it comes to people who don't know me, I rarely lash out or get angry. It's as if I put on my 'working cap' for work and when I'm not working and it's off, I tend to be quiet, shy and not very talkative.

> *'Stoicism: the endurance of pain and hardship without the display of feeling and without complaint.'*
> OXFORD ENGLISH DICTIONARY

This was the problem I found. The outside world was getting the best of me, my energy and my positive thoughts and feelings, yet my family and friends seemed to be getting the leftovers, which wasn't much.

If I could summarise stoicism in one sentence, it would be a philosophy that teaches you to control what you can control and to let go of what you can't control:

> *'Life is 10% what happens to you and 90% how you deal with it.'*
> CHARLES R. SWINDOLL

When we wake up in the morning, we cannot control what we're going to see or what is going to happen to us that day. One minute we could be minding our own business, having a glorious day, and the next we get a phone call to say someone we love has passed away.

What stoicism teaches you to do is to control your mind and choose your behaviour, and it's based upon four cardinal virtues:

> **Prudence** – The ability to govern oneself by the use of reason

> **Courage** – The choice and willingness to confront agony, pain, danger, uncertainty or intimidation

> **Temperance** – Moderation or voluntary self-restraint

> **Justice** – The moderation or median between selfishness and selflessness – between having more and having less than one's fair share

As you can imagine from the last chapter, I had figured out that my balance between selfishness and selflessness was out of whack, and when I read the four virtues of stoic philosophy it hit me like a ton of bricks.

THE PARADOX OF PRUDENCE

Courage, temperance and justice are part of a scale, and prudence is the judge of these three things. Prudence is not an action – it is the knowledge of where on the scale these things are in your life:

> Courageous acts can also be cowardly ones depending on their judgement on the scale

> Having too much temperance can be just as damaging as overindulging

Going back to the principles of polarity, each of these three virtues falls on a scale and prudence decides where these things are on the scale.

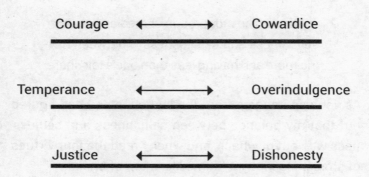

The Three Virtue Scales

Using the paradox of prudence enabled me to understand, much like the principle of polarity, that to get out of the hole I was in I needed to be honest with myself and understand where I fell on these three virtue scales:

> ❯ **Courage** – There were a lot of courageous things I was doing in my life. The pain, agony and uncertainty of building my body and business were something that I knew quite well and I was high up on the scale with them, but when it came to my relationships, I was a coward. I would do anything to avoid pain or uncertainty by trying to numb the pain or create certainty by cutting it off. I

would fail miserably to connect with others emotionally as I thought it was weak to show others my pain and suffering. What it actually did was make me human.

> **Temperance** – I have high temperance in a lot of situations. I rarely overindulge in things such as food and mindless entertainment, which enables me to maintain a healthy physique and a productive working life. I understand well the importance of not over-training the body with exercise, owing to the law of diminishing returns, and not overindulging the brain with mindless Netflix crap.

In other places I was overindulging and needed to practise moderation and self-restraint, particularly in my use of social media and my time and energy spent on strangers, customers and clients. This needed to be moderated so that I could give the things for which these people pay me to my family; these are my time, my energy and my attention.

> **Justice** – I have to re-balance my levels of selfishness and unselfishness and start saying no to strangers so that I can focus my time, energy and attention on the people I love.

When people think of stoicism, they think of a person who doesn't feel. They believe that you need to express your emotion on your face so that others can understand how you feel. This is a feedback loop for others to see how they need to respond to you. And this is my problem with it.

Most people's reactions can be read the wrong way. Responding to people's emotions would assume that we are logical creatures. When people display emotion in person or even in the comments section on Instagram, it would be only logical to interpret that as a sign that you need to respond appropriately.

If someone gets angry in person or online, you need to apologise or get angry back. If someone starts to sabotage something of yours, you feel the need to sabotage something back. This logic is flawed, as we are not logical creatures. We are emotional creatures and we back it up with logic.

We naturally want to fight fire with fire in these situations because it's only right that if someone does us wrong, we get them back. But if someone gets angry in person or online, it's important to understand that those who shout hate are secretly asking for help.

If someone starts to tear down the castle you're building, it's usually because they are jealous or resentful of your castle because they are struggling to build theirs. Instead of retaliating, reach out to them and show them how they can build their own castle.

When it comes to stoicism, it's not that the person feels nothing; they feel *everything*, and instead of responding with emotion, they use reasoning and respond with logic.

We can't choose our emotions. We all feel guilt, anger, shame, jealousy, resentment and envy. These are subconscious thoughts. What we can choose are the conscious actions that we respond with.

This is much harder than is explained above, as there are times when it would be good to show some emotion. If you're going through a hard time with your relationship and you aren't letting the person you love know that it's affecting you, this could create the point of no return in your relationship. I expressed my pain and suffering in my own case, as this was required not only for Anna's understanding but for mine too.

There are two mental models from stoicism I use each day that increase my focus, productivity and motivation: Memento Mori and A View From Above.

MEMENTO MORI

Memento Mori is a Latin phrase meaning 'Remember that you have to die'.

People don't want to talk about death, even if it is the one guarantee that we have in our lives. If you don't wake up every day remembering that one day all this will be gone, you forget to actually live.

Every day remind yourself that your loved ones will pass away, your brothers, your sisters, your sons and your daughters – just stop for a second and think about these things. This thinking allows me to appreciate the people I love more and gives me the mindset that allows me to face my fears, take risks and push forward. It also allows me to 'down tools' and be there with my family more. The last thing you want to have on your deathbed is regret.

A VIEW FROM ABOVE

I was in the British Army for seven years and worked as a contract worker in Nairobi, Kenya and Somalia. I have seen first-hand how we should appreciate the little things in life, such as clean water and walking around without worrying about getting shot or blown up.

Unless you have been in war-torn countries it's hard to appreciate the simple things in life and not get annoyed when your phone battery dies halfway through updating your Instagram feed. A view from above will help with this.

Imagine looking down on yourself from 100 feet in the air; now go higher and imagine looking down on yourself from the clouds. You're looking pretty small now. Now go higher, let's say to the international space station, and then further, maybe to the moon, and look down on this pale blue dot we call home.

In the grander scheme of things, our battery dying on our phone really doesn't matter, nor does anything we care about when compared to the problems on and off our planet. No one cares except you, which is why you shouldn't waste the little time you have on this planet in a negative state of mind and should do more things that make you happy.

TASK

Write down the three virtue scales and note both the positive and negative things that you are currently doing in your life for each of them. Ask yourself if you are on the right track or whether something needs changing.

Take courage, for example, and ask yourself if you are facing your fears and being honest with yourself about the things you need to do in your life. When it comes to temperance, are you overly restrictive with your nutrition and exercise or do you need to adopt more discipline with these? With justice, are you being there too much for others and need to focus more on yourself?

Next, do your Meltdown Management Scale and mark each one from 1 to 5.

Chapter 3 scoring	
Health (mental and physical)	
1 – Poor and in desperate need of improvement	
2 – Below average	
3 – Average	
4 – Above average	
5 – Elite	
Wealth (financial and social)	
1 – Struggling with finances and in desperate need of improvement	
2 – Below average	
3 – Average	
4 – Above average	
5 – An abundance of financial and social wealth	
Productivity	
1 – Struggling to get even the smallest task completed each day	
2 – Below average	
3 – Average	
4 – Above average	
5 – A productivity machine	
Connectivity (physical and emotional)	
1 – Barely connect with anyone physically on a daily basis	
2 – Connect with people physically once a week	
3 – Connect with people physically 2–3 times a week	
4 – Connect with people physically and emotionally 3–5 times a week	
5 – Connect with people physically and emotionally every day	
Total	
Average	

RUNNING AVERAGES

Ch. 1	Ch. 2	Ch. 3

CHAPTER 4

THE ATTITUDE OF GRATITUDE

Never underestimate the powerful effect that the simple daily practice of appreciating what you already have can have on your mental well-being.

From 2003 to 2009 I was a soldier in the British Army and between 2011 and 2012 I worked as a security advisor. In both of these jobs I worked in some of the most war-torn countries in the world.

> 'Do not spoil what you have by desiring what you have not. Remember that what you now have was once among the things you only hoped for.'
>
> EPICTETUS

One of the biggest wake-up calls for me was when I was based in Mogadishu, Somalia back in 2011. The Somali people are very kind and generous and one thing I noticed was just how much they smiled. There was a war going on and some of these people had had everything taken away from them, including their loved ones, yet they were smiling because they had food and shelter and got to live for another day. This made me think really deeply and prompted me to consider a lot of things about worry, sadness and overwhelm and how each of them affects us in everyday life.

We have the world literally at our fingertips now… we can dig into our pockets and take out a device that gives us the tools to get skinny, rich and happy at the touch of a button. Life should now be one big party as there is so much abundance in the world. But what seemed to be the solution to our problems has now become the problem.

When I was younger, there were only about five TV channels before my mum and dad got Sky TV. I remember the film premiere being a massive thing on a Friday night, and the whole family would gather round to watch whatever was on.

Last night I spent twenty-five minutes on Netflix filtering through the 9,796 films that it has to offer, trying to decide what to watch. I've just wasted twenty-five minutes of my life because I don't want to watch something that might waste my time or that I might not like… this in itself wastes an abundance of time on decision making.

That daily twenty-five-minute problem that most people experience, compounded over a year, is 152 hours of wasted time. That's almost a week of my life wasted getting anxiety and overwhelm over what to choose to 'relax' with on TV.

Another situation like this I remember was before the arrival of the iPod, when you had CDs in your car. I would have one or two CDs in the car and play them to death until someone bought me a new CD. I didn't mind listening to the same twenty tracks over and over again, and it became quite therapeutic after a while.

In came the iPod and I remember buying a car kit for it that suddenly enabled me to have 20,000 songs at the touch of a button. I now had so many albums and songs that I didn't know what to listen to.

The issue comes down to choice, and there are many correlations with this anxiety and overwhelm, much of which comes down to one simple word... comparison.

It has never been easier to compare what we currently have with what others have. This affects our decision making and

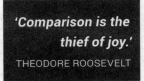

'Comparison is the thief of joy.'
THEODORE ROOSEVELT

choices more and more, especially online. I am seeing this with FOMO (Fear of Missing Out). FOMO is a form of social anxiety characterised by a desire to always be connected to what others are doing.

Two huge psychological needs of human beings, especially when it comes to motivation, are relatedness and connectedness. We like to surround ourselves with people with similar interests and we like to connect with others and talk. Before the internet, in order for us to do this, we would need to get up, get dressed and leave the house.

Now we can sit in our pyjamas, unlock our phones and instantly be connected to billions of people. This is the problem... if you're not on your phone or the internet for just fifteen minutes, you feel as if you're missing out on something (it's not surprising, as every sixty seconds on Facebook 510,000 comments are posted, 293,000 statuses are updated and 136,000 photos are uploaded).

It's because of this fear that we spend so much time connecting, comparing and talking online that we forget to connect and talk with real people and spend any time whatsoever away from our mobile phones.

What is the answer to this? Something called JOMO and, most importantly, gratitude.

JOMO (JOY OF MISSING OUT)

JOMO is one of the best things you can condition your mind to do, and it's the complete opposite of FOMO.

Each year since 2017 I have removed myself from social media and gone away on holiday for an entire week. At first, I feel FOMO creeping in and worry I'll miss out on something big, or that when I switch on my phone again the hundreds of thousands of people who follow me will have disappeared.

Two things have happened since I have done this:

> It took me less than fifteen minutes to catch up with the world

> Views of and engagement with my content increased in the following week (mainly because my body and mind were completely refreshed with new ideas)

There is a certain joy to missing out on things, and switching off for one day a week and one week a year has seen my mood and wellbeing increased, which then makes it easier the next time I do it.

There is so much abundance in the world these days that you have to remember you aren't going to see and experience it all in your lifetime. An interesting fact is that it would take you three million years to download all the information on the internet, let alone read it, so no one has time for that.

Pick and choose the things that matter to you in your life. For those that really don't matter, learn to take some joy in missing things, as it allows you to do things that you really want to do.

The reason I have said so much in this chapter about feeling anxious and overwhelmed is that many of these things can be improved by going back in time to a place where the things we now take for granted didn't exist. We need to strip things back and spend a little time every day reflecting on just how awesome our lives currently are.

I am typing this from my home office while my two children sleep upstairs. I have a great business and a loving wife to whom I am now more connected than ever. If I'm hungry I can walk ten paces to my big American fridge and pull out whatever I desire to eat, and if it's not there I can get in one of my two cars and drive to the supermarket to get whatever it is I desire. I want to be clear that I'm saying this not to brag, far from it! You will have things in your life that you love and appreciate as much as this.

Whatever they are, write them down and remind yourself of them daily.

It is non-negotiable that every single day we must take two minutes to remind ourselves just how incredible life is these days and make sure that we never fail to do so. Having an attitude of gratitude, and enjoying missing out on the abundance of things that I could be doing but choose not to, has helped me reduce the impact of many of these thoughts and feelings I have had over the years, which has enabled me to enjoy a much simpler and more rewarding life.

TASK

I challenge you to practise the attitude of gratitude for seven days straight and I'm going to help you do it without missing a single day with this little 'habit hack'.

Creating a new habit is much easier if you tie it to an existing daily habit, and the best one is when you brush your teeth.

Grab a sticky note and write on it 'three things you are grateful for today' and then stick it on the mirror in your bathroom or in plain sight of where you brush your teeth each day.

As you are brushing your teeth, take those two minutes to think about the things you currently have in your life and how awesome it is. I promise you that when you start doing this morning and night, you will start to notice the difference.

Next, you need to do your Meltdown Management Scale and mark each one from 1 to 5.

Chapter 4 scoring	
Health (mental and physical)	
1 – Poor and in desperate need of improvement	
2 – Below average	
3 – Average	
4 – Above average	
5 – Elite	
Wealth (financial and social)	
1 – Struggling with finances and in desperate need of improvement	
2 – Below average	
3 – Average	
4 – Above average	
5 – An abundance of financial and social wealth	
Productivity	
1 – Struggling to get even the smallest task completed each day	
2 – Below average	
3 – Average	
4 – Above average	
5 – A productivity machine	
Connectivity (physical and emotional)	
1 – Barely connect with anyone physically on a daily basis	
2 – Connect with people physically once a week	
3 – Connect with people physically 2–3 times a week	
4 – Connect with people physically and emotionally 3–5 times a week	
5 – Connect with people physically and emotionally every day	
Total	
Average	

RUNNING AVERAGES

Ch. 1	Ch. 2	Ch. 3	Ch. 4

MENTAL MODELS

Our brains are complex things, and over the years I've delved deep into my own reasonings and judgements. We have many different coping strategies to deal with what life throws at us; some of these can be good and some can be bad.

To better understand mental models, look at your brain as a Rubik's cube. If I gave you one and asked you to solve it, you would play around with it for many hours. You might even manage to solve a couple of the sides but eventually you would give up because it is far too complex.

Imagine that I taught you the specific methods to solve the Rubik's cube and that when you put a certain colour in a certain place you are only about thirty moves away from solving it. These moves are called algorithms, and mental models are algorithms for the brain.

You can spend years trying to solve things, but if I chuck a few mental models at you, which I am going to do in this chapter, it will help you to solve the puzzle of your mind.

SELECTIVE HEARING

One of the mental models I like to focus on is selective hearing, and I'll give you a better understanding of this with a little scenario. Say you're at a noisy party and you're speaking to a friend. Your brain has the ability to block out the noise of other people speaking around you and focus on what your friend is saying. This is known as the cocktail party effect and was first put forward by British cognitive scientist Edward Colin Cherry. It has a strong correlation with confirmation bias, which is the tendency to search for, interpret, favour and recall information in a way that confirms one's pre-existing beliefs or hypotheses.

As you can see, this kind of selective hearing can be a double-edged sword. If you use it for good, it allows you to block out other people's negativity and not get offended by words and opinions. The bad side of this is that you hear from others what you want to hear or you ignore other people's well-intentioned advice.

When you're having a discussion with someone who questions your beliefs or identity, you get angry and emotional, and once emotions take over, all logic goes out the window. This happens

> *'You can't see your own reflection in boiling water.'*
> ANON

a lot with people's health, wealth and relationships. When we're suffering with these, it feels as if people are attacking us or pointing the finger.

It has always been the case that more attention and focus have been on the negative than the positive, mainly down to how our brains are wired. I've seen a lot of this online with what's called 'call-out culture'. This is a type of public shaming used to hold other people and groups accountable for behaviour thought to be problematic, usually on social media.

The trouble with call-out culture is that you don't need to be right in your opinions for it to have an effect. If you have a good following and have enough people who believe in what you're saying, a lot of people will jump on board.

This is usually a recipe for disaster if you're the person building up your audience with this kind of tactic. You become a dancing monkey for others who will encourage you to repeat this behaviour for their own enjoyment and benefit – certainly not something that is going to be good for your mental health in the long run.

How can you use selective attention in your own life for good? It takes a lot of time and a lot of practice, but it all starts with one thing: being brutally honest with yourself. If you are listening to or reading something that you don't agree with or feel is a personal attack on you, you need to ask yourself why you think that is so.

In the previous chapters, I mentioned the scale of courage and cowardice and many people not realising that these things are on the same scale. The subject in question would indicate where on the scale you are.

With my risk-taking in business and my achievements I would consider myself to be pretty high on the courage scale, but when it comes to dealing with emotions in relationships, I would have to put myself pretty high on the cowardice scale.

Being brutally honest not only with your strengths but also with your weaknesses is not an easy thing to do, but it is a step in the right direction to understanding how you're going to improve.

To grow, we need to accept that we are flawed individuals and that most people are just waking up each day and trying their best. We're social animals and we want to have attention focused on us, which can be done in many different ways, both positive and negative.

HANLON'S RAZOR

Another mental model I use on a daily basis is called Hanlon's razor, which states: 'Never attribute to malice that which can be explained by stupidity.'

A great way of explaining this is to imagine yourself in a car, and as you're driving on the motorway someone suddenly cuts you up. Enraged by this person's attitude and malice, you put your foot on the gas, undertake them and drive up to the side of their car to give them a piece of your mind.

But then you notice in the car a little old lady and you suddenly realise that the reason she cut you up is probably because her eyesight isn't as good as it used to be and it was an accident. You immediately calm down and carry on with your journey.

In life people have a tendency to think the world revolves around them and that a lot of people are out there to sabotage their success. Newsflash: they are not. People wake up every morning drowning in their problems, and when you're drowning in anything the last thing you're thinking about is other people; you are just flailing your arms around trying to survive.

This mental model has enabled me to deal with customers, clients and employees much better by understanding that the Earth orbits around the Sun and not around me. It has enabled me to walk a mile in the other person's shoes from time to time and to consider their actions not to be malicious but because they are struggling to breathe and decision making has become difficult for them.

Ego can be an asset and can enable you to achieve great and powerful things, but if it is not kept in check it can be a recipe for disaster. It's your ego that kicks in and makes you think that people are out to get you and that there are people plotting and planning their next move to destroy what you are trying to build. What Hanlon's Razor conditions your mind to believe is that most of the time this is not true.

It's a practice that you need to strengthen daily by constantly looking at the real reasons that people do things, not what you have fabricated in your mind.

THE NORM OF RECIPROCITY

The next mental model I use a lot in my business and personal life is 'the norm of reciprocity': 'Give and forget, receive and remember.'

The norm of reciprocity requires that we repay in kind what another has done for us. If you're giving people gifts every single day, it is only a matter of time before you start to see some of that come back to you. This has a strong correlation to the Indian religious concept of Karma, which explains this reciprocity effect in a better way. It's a cause and effect where if you do good things to people, good things will happen to you, and if you do bad things to people, bad things will happen to you.

One thing I want to add is that people have a tendency to fight fire with fire, especially online, so if someone says something negative to you, you naturally want to return the favour and say something negative back. Over the years I have practised fighting negativity with positivity, and when someone has said something hurtful to me online, I have said something positive to them in return.

It's hard for someone to be mean to you when you are being so kind to them, and it's always important to understand that.

PARETO PRINCIPLE

The Pareto principle, also known as the 80/20 law, was originally named after Italian economist Vilfredo Pareto. He noticed that 80% of the land in Italy was owned by 20% of the population. What the Pareto principle basically states is that roughly 80% of the effects come from 20% of the causes. For example, Microsoft noticed that by fixing the top 20% of the bugs in their software, 80% of the related errors and crashes in a given system would be eliminated.[4]

How can we apply this Pareto principle in our own lives? It's by applying the 20% of fundamental focuses to our body, brain and business that is going to produce 80% of the results.

When it comes to your body, if you focus on your calories, your steps and your sleep, this will have a greater effect on your body than anything else you do. When it comes to your brain, focusing on doing fewer things and

---

4 www.crn.com/news/security/18821726/microsofts-ceo-80-20-rule-applies-to-bugs-not-just-features.htm

having less stuff will have a significant impact on your productivity in business. When you focus on creating just one or two incredible products for certain clients rather than focusing on catering for anyone and everyone, your business will start to grow.

We need to look at the 20% of things we do daily that produce 80% of the results and start to understand this better if we want to make massive waves with our success.

TASK

There are many different mental models and algorithms that you can use to improve your body, brain and business. Think about the ones that I have discussed in this chapter and how you can apply them to your life. When you focus on yourself and those things that matter, and condition yourself not to get caught up in the opinions of others, life becomes better.

When you focus on giving gifts and delivering value each day, it eventually benefits you. Lastly, when you focus on the 20% of things that actually make a significant impact on your body, brain and business, life becomes less overwhelming and you start to really push the needle forward.

Next, you need to do your Meltdown Management Scale and mark each one from 1 to 5.

Chapter 5 scoring	
Health (mental and physical)	
1 – Poor and in desperate need of improvement	
2 – Below average	
3 – Average	
4 – Above average	
5 – Elite	
Wealth (financial and social)	
1 – Struggling with finances and in desperate need of improvement	
2 – Below average	
3 – Average	
4 – Above average	
5 – An abundance of financial and social wealth	
Productivity	
1 – Struggling to get even the smallest task completed each day	
2 – Below average	
3 – Average	
4 – Above average	
5 – A productivity machine	
Connectivity (physical and emotional)	
1 – Barely connect with anyone physically on a daily basis	
2 – Connect with people physically once a week	
3 – Connect with people physically 2–3 times a week	
4 – Connect with people physically and emotionally 3–5 times a week	
5 – Connect with people physically and emotionally every day	
Total	
Average	

RUNNING AVERAGES

Ch. 1	Ch. 2	Ch. 3	Ch. 4	Ch. 5

CHAPTER 6

THE COLD-WATER CURE

I was in the local swimming pool getting ready to go for a morning swim and as I approached the showers an older gentleman stopped me and said: 'You'll want to give those showers a miss today son, they're freezing cold.' I looked at him and smiled as I stepped under the ice-cold shower and proceeded to rinse my hair, as the cold water barely made me flinch. A weird look came over the man's face as he wondered how on earth I could just walk into a shower as cold as that as if it was nothing. Well... three months ago I probably would have taken heed of his advice.

> 'The cure for anything is salt water: sweat, tears or the sea.'
>
> ISAK DINESEN

If anything is going wrong in your life and you're looking for a way to improve it, rather than trying to mask the issue with drugs, sex or alcohol, give one of the above a try first:

> Hit the gym and get a good sweat on; the endorphin release will make you feel better.

> Let it all out with someone close to you, sometimes turning yourself into a blubbering wreck and getting all that pent-up emotion out might help you smile.

> Go for a walk, preferably by the sea, and if you really want your mood to improve, get in the sea.

I've been walking by the sea for the past five years and I'm lucky to live just ten minutes from it down on the Sussex coast. This year has been different as I said to myself that I wanted to start swimming in the morning. There was just one problem: it was coming to the end of January and I could not muster the courage to strip off and jump in for fear of catching a cold. I wanted to overcome this thought process and try to find a way of building up to this jump in the ice-cold sea... in came the cold showers.

I had seen a lot about cold showers from Wim Hof, known as the Iceman. For those of you who don't know who he is, he has broken multiple world records with his ability to withstand freezing temperatures, which includes swimming under ice and a barefoot half marathon on ice and snow. Seeing the Iceman and others talk about the cold and its benefits intrigued me and I wanted to know more to find out how it could help me.

'THE COLD SHOWER CHALLENGE'

When you know you're about to have a cold shower, you are filled with doubt and anticipation. The thought of freezing water on your skin makes you think of a million reasons not to do it. If I was going to have cold showers, I needed to be consistent with them and to hold myself accountable too.

One of the huge benefits of having a large social media audience is that you can hold yourself accountable to them. Over the years I've done this with my bodybuilding shows, my charity events and even with writing my books and courses. I let my audience know that I was going to do a 'Cold Shower Challenge' in February. The challenge was that I would have a cold shower every day without fail and that I would film it every day to make sure that I did.

My first cold shower was an interesting one. I set my countdown timer to thirty seconds, pressed record on my camera to film it and jumped under the freezing water. The minute I stepped in, it took my breath away. I kept up the deep breathing which I had seen others do, and thirty seconds felt like three hours before my timer started to beep and I quickly moved the shower temperature from cold to hot. Boom! First shower done and this incredible feeling of endorphins, achievement and wellbeing took over in my body. This is kind of cool, I said to myself, looking forward to the next day.

The next day came and I had forgotten that awesome feeling I had at the end of yesterday's session. I immediately started to think about that ice-cold water on my skin and how uncomfortable I felt when I put that shower on. If it hadn't been for the fact that I was challenging myself and recording it for social media, I could easily have skipped today's session, but like yesterday, after some heavy breathing and what felt like hours passing by, my timer beeped and I flicked the temperature back to a nice hot shower. Once again endorphins were released, I had a feeling of accomplishment and I felt amazing.

COMMITMENT AND CONSISTENCY

I persisted with the challenge and after about two weeks, something incredible happened on the fourteenth or fifteenth shower. I started to feel the cold less and actually looked forward to each shower. I was starting to adapt to the cold so much that cold showers were developing into a new habit.

I learned a lot from my cold shower challenge both physically and mentally, and here are my take aways.

Like a lot of things in our lives that produce a huge return on invest-ment (exercise, writing, cold showers), you have to do these things every single day without fail for at least two weeks before you start to see the benefits.

> *'Commitment is doing the thing you said you were going to do long after the mood in which you said it has passed.'*
>
> LES BROWN

For a new habit to take hold, it doesn't need to be enjoyable but it does need to be essential for your physical and mental wellbeing. Once you start to see that it is having a positive impact on your life, it becomes hard *not to do it*. I can't think of anyone who actually looks forward to brushing their teeth every day but you know how essen-tial it is, so you do it.

When you spend enough time exercising, not only do you see the positive return on your body but you think more clearly, become more productive and overall feel so much better about yourself and your life.

When you commit to writing or journalling for just five minutes every day, within two weeks you will have greater insight into your problems and a huge boost in mental wellbeing.

When you commit to doing a cold shower challenge for an entire month, it will only take half that time to realise its impact on your productivity and wellbeing. For me, the cold showers were a stepping stone and were getting me mentally and physically prepared for the real thing I wanted to do, and that was the cold sea dips.

It's March now and I'm getting together everything I need for my first cold sea dip. The water temperature is a fresh eight degrees, which as a temperature guide is classed as 'freezing'.

I change into some swim shorts and brace myself for what is going to be an incredible experience. I walk down to the water, which immediately feels a lot colder on my feet than any cold shower I have done, wade in up to waist height and mentally prepare myself to fully submerge my body: 3... 2... 1... Go!

I jump right in and immediately experience jolting gasps of air as I try to control this insane drop in the temperature of my body. I cannot think of anything apart from trying to breathe and adapt to its ice-cold temperature. Thirty seconds pass and the insane cold starts to fade. My body feels warmer and I'm grinning like a Cheshire cat for no apparent reason. This is what open water swimmers call 'the cold-water high'. Rushes of endorphins flood the body and you feel incredible!

It didn't take me long to realise that these cold-water dips are life-changing for both your physical and mental wellbeing. There are many studies that show a range of physical and mental benefits of cold-water exposure, though a lot of them are speculative as randomised controlled trials are lacking.

For this reason, I am going to relate some personal anecdotes from using cold-water exposure most days since February 2019 and how it can have a positive impact on your life should you add it to your routine.

One of the most powerful things you can train your mind to do is to do something even though you don't want to do it. This is because so many people rely on motivation to take action on things in their lives, but the trouble with this is that you will not take action unless you are motivated. If you are committed to something, it shouldn't matter whether you want to do it or not; it is a necessity in your life and you must do it.

During the first month of sea dips, I would look out of the window and see that the weather was not very nice. I would then immediately tell myself that 'maybe you shouldn't go in the sea today'. This was my mind playing tricks on me and trying to convince me not to have that incredible endorphin rush I remembered getting each time I go in and out. I realised that when my brain tells me that I shouldn't do a sea dip, that day is the most important day to do so.

The biggest enemy of progress is ourselves, and if we can convince ourselves not to do something, we will not do it. The daily struggle between ignoring my head's advice and doing it anyway was building a stronger, more productive mindset, which has allowed me to stay committed to my morning sea dips.

The first of my 'cold-water cure' tips is: 'Do something you don't want to do every single morning.' This could be going to the gym, taking a cold shower, writing for five minutes each morning. Commit to doing it whether you want to or not and this will help you build an incredibly powerful mindset.

My second 'cold-water cure' takeaway is that there are two things that we know have a positive impact on our life: breathing and meditation. Taking controlled breaths can help reduce stress and improve wellbeing, and so can meditation. Both of these can be hard to do, and I have personally struggled to do them consistently. Because of cold sea dips, that has now changed.

When you jump into ice-cold water your mind becomes clear and you can't think of anything apart from trying to breathe. You take big breaths and have an empty mind for two to three minutes at a time.

Cold-water therapy is the gift that keeps on giving! You get the benefit from the exposure to the cold with a release of endorphins and you get the state of wellbeing that comes from breathing and meditation, all rolled into one.

From my short time with cold-water exposure I have found such a huge return on my physical and mental wellbeing that it is now a fundamental part of my habits and routines.

TASK

My challenge for you is to do a twenty-one-day cold shower challenge. Your task is to get into an ice-cold shower for thirty seconds, breathing deeply, before switching it to hot. If you want to make it a little easier, have a warm shower first, switch it to cold and then go back to hot.

It took me fourteen days to see the real benefits of cold-water exposure, so challenging yourself for twenty-one days is a great amount of time to commit to.

Next, you need to do your Meltdown Management Scale and mark each one from 1 to 5.

Chapter 6 scoring	
Health (mental and physical)	
1 – Poor and in desperate need of improvement	
2 – Below average	
3 – Average	
4 – Above average	
5 – Elite	
Wealth (financial and social)	
1 – Struggling with finances and in desperate need of improvement	
2 – Below average	
3 – Average	
4 – Above average	
5 – An abundance of financial and social wealth	
Productivity	
1 – Struggling to get even the smallest task completed each day	
2 – Below average	
3 – Average	
4 – Above average	
5 – A productivity machine	
Connectivity (physical and emotional)	
1 – Barely connect with anyone physically on a daily basis	
2 – Connect with people physically once a week	
3 – Connect with people physically 2–3 times a week	
4 – Connect with people physically and emotionally 3–5 times a week	
5 – Connect with people physically and emotionally every day	
Total	
Average	

RUNNING AVERAGES

Ch. 1	Ch. 2	Ch. 3	Ch. 4	Ch. 5	Ch. 6

THE EISENHOWER DECISION MATRIX

This was quoted by former US President Dwight D Eisenhower in a 1954 speech to the Second Assembly of the World Council of Churches.

> *'I have two kinds of problems, the urgent and the important. The urgent are not important, and the important are never urgent.'*
>
> DR J ROSCOE MILLER

President Eisenhower was an incredibly successful man. He was president of the United States not once but twice, and he was also a five-star General in the US Army and General of the victorious forces in Europe during the Second World War. He was also President of Columbia University. It is safe to say that Eisenhower was a busy and productive man.

Because of this quote, the Eisenhower Decision Matrix was formed. It is made up of four categories in which you segment your tasks for the day, the week and the month:

> Do – Urgent and important. You do these tasks immediately.

> Defer – Important, but not urgent. You schedule these tasks for later.

> Delegate – Urgent, but not important. You delegate these tasks if possible.

> Delete – Neither urgent nor important. You eliminate these tasks if possible.

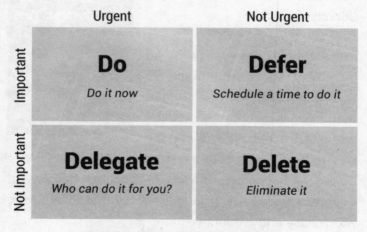

The Eisenhower Decision Matrix

Do

I heard an interview with Will Smith asking about the key to his success. He said he was aware that he was world-class at only a few things, and anything that takes him away from those things needs to be done by someone else.

From day to day we do so many things that other people could do for us, yet our pride gets in the way and we don't want to ask for help or hire someone. One of the most important things to look at is how much you value your time per hour, and there is a pretty simple equation to find this out:

1. If you had to charge someone for an hour of additional work that you really don't want to do, what would you charge them for that hour? Write down your answer.

2. You receive a £100 gift certificate but to claim it you must wait in line for a period of time to get it. What's the maximum amount of time you would wait (up to 180 minutes)? Write down your answer.

3. You have a four-hour task this weekend that you neither love nor hate doing. There is an option of using a paid tool that will re-duce that time from four hours to just four

minutes. How much would you be willing to pay to use this tool? Write down your answer.

4. You are travelling somewhere by train and you have the option to upgrade to an express train that will save an hour of your time. How much would you be willing to pay for that train upgrade? Write down your answer.

Do you have your answers? Good. Now it's time to work out how much you think your time is worth per hour:

> If you answered £100 to question 1, this is because you believe your time is worth £100 an hour

> If you put thirty minutes on question 2, this would mean you value your time at £200 an hour

> If you thought you would pay £100 to access the tool that will save you almost four hours of time, this shows you value your time at £25 an hour

> If you would pay £50 for the upgrade of your train ticket to save an hour, this would mean you value your time at £50 an hour

Now we add up all those totals and divide the answer by four to get an average. This would mean that you value your time at £93.75 per hour.

When it comes to your Do box, it's important to remember that hourly rate (or start thinking differently about how much you value your time). Understand that if there are currently any jobs that are taking you away from your work that earns you let's say £95 per hour, you really should not be doing them unless you enjoy doing them. What I mean by this is that you can pay somebody else to clean your house, but if you really enjoy doing it, and it allows you to listen to some music and relax, then by all means keep doing it.

DEFER

We have a natural tendency to look at our to-do list and do the most interesting and exciting things first. This makes sense to our brains as we want to feel stimulated and motivated. What we have to do is to change our mindset so that we ask: which are the most important tasks that are going to help push the needle forward? These might not be the most interesting tasks, but they are certainly the most important.

I like to prioritise my Do and Defer boxes into three categories. Number 1 is the most important and needs to be done today.

Number 2 is deferred but it needs to be done within three days, and number 3 is also deferred but needs to be done by the end of the week. Remember that your deferred list should still be a list of things that only you can do, because the tasks are more expensive than what you earn per hour.

DELEGATE

One of the hardest things to do in business and in life is to trust other people to do work for you. This could be cooking and cleaning when these are tasks you can do just fine, or doing day-to-day admin tasks in your business because doing them is so ingrained in you that you think no one can do them better than you.

Understand that this pattern of thinking is losing you money.

> 'Hire people who are better than you are, then leave them to get on with it... Look for people who will aim for the remarkable, who will not settle for the routine.'
> DAVID OGILVY

Many small business owners, including myself, are very controlling. We have a certain way of doing things and if people don't do them our way, we get annoyed and frustrated.

What we forget is that the reason we are so good at doing these tasks is because we are so used to doing them that they have become built-in habits on autopilot. When we see other people doing these tasks, it's like allowing someone else to steer your car and you immediately become that backseat driver telling them when to signal and manoeuvre.

That is not how you learned to drive. You learned from making mistakes and from hours of repetition and focus. You need to allow others to make a few small mistakes so that they learn what to do, or give them some advice on the mistakes that you made when you first started out in these tasks, so they can avoid them altogether.

I've hired and fired a lot of people in my time, and the quotes you hear today are the same ones you have always heard: 'if you pay peanuts you get monkeys' and 'if you think hiring a professional is expensive, try hiring an amateur'.

It takes time to find good people but when you do, pay them well and be confident in delegating tasks to them so you can get on with your world-class work.

DELETE

I have a big social media following and doing lots of cool things with my business allows me to have the freedom and flexibility to work on many different and exciting projects. I've made the mistake of saying yes to too many things that have taken me away from my world-class focus, all because they seemed like fun ideas to pursue.

> 'I'm actually as proud of the things we haven't done as the things I have done. Innovation is saying no to 1,000 things.'
>
> STEVE JOBS

The two biggest things you need to practise are saying no to opportunities and learning how to completely delete tasks from your to-do list. If you have a to-do list and you look at it right now, I can guarantee that there are things on it that you have committed yourself to that you really didn't want to do but were too afraid to say no. You worry that saying no will annoy the other person, but when handled correctly this can often be mitigated. This all comes back to people respecting your time; and if they don't, why should you respect theirs?

In the past, I've seen people take this delete part a little too seriously (myself included) and start deleting things that they think are not good uses of their time but actually are *investments* of their time, for example:

> *Investing* in your relationships with the people you love

> *Investing* in activities that make you forget you have a mobile phone

> *Investing* in holidays to give your brain a break

These things should never be deleted – controlled and considered, yes, but never deleted.

TASK

It's time to start implementing the Eisenhower Decision Matrix and start sectioning your to-do list. Write down a list of everything that needs to be done this week (that includes cleaning, meetings, and commitments you have with family and friends).

Write next to each item Do, Defer, Delegate or Delete. If it is a Do, it's a priority that must be completed today. If it is a Defer, it needs to be added to your diary as a priority for later in the week or month. If it's a Delegate, add it to the to-do list of your staff or hired help. And if it is a Delete, make sure you handle it correctly if other people's time and energy are involved.

Next, you need to do your Meltdown Management Scale and mark each one from 1 to 5.

Chapter 7 scoring	
Health (mental and physical)	
1 – Poor and in desperate need of improvement	
2 – Below average	
3 – Average	
4 – Above average	
5 – Elite	
Wealth (financial and social)	
1 – Struggling with finances and in desperate need of improvement	
2 – Below average	
3 – Average	
4 – Above average	
5 – An abundance of financial and social wealth	
Productivity	
1 – Struggling to get even the smallest task completed each day	
2 – Below average	
3 – Average	
4 – Above average	
5 – A productivity machine	
Connectivity (physical and emotional)	
1 – Barely connect with anyone physically on a daily basis	
2 – Connect with people physically once a week	
3 – Connect with people physically 2–3 times a week	
4 – Connect with people physically and emotionally 3–5 times a week	
5 – Connect with people physically and emotionally every day	
Total	
Average	

RUNNING AVERAGES

Ch. 1	Ch. 2	Ch. 3	Ch. 4	Ch. 5	Ch. 6	Ch. 7

ONE CHAPTER PER DAY

Committing to one single act each day can compound exponentially in the space of a year.

Imagine that it's January and this year you have decided that you're going to go all out on self-development, or as some people call it, 'shelf-development'. You ask me for a list of the best books in the world that have changed my life. The next day I come back with a giant stack of books, thirty-six to be precise. I slam them down on your desk and say, 'There you go, enjoy.' It can be a little overwhelming looking at so many books. Where on earth do you start?

You grab one of the books and start reading. Four weeks pass and you've made a great dent in the pile, managing five books in January. You get a little bit out of routine in February and work has taken its toll, but you still manage to get another four books in.

March comes along and the all-in mentality you had in January is starting to fade. Reading so many books is exhausting, and you've forgotten what the first five books you read at the start of the year were. You just about manage to scrape through two books by the end of this month.

It's April now and you only managed to complete one of the books this month. You look at this giant pile of books still on your desk and count them – twenty-four books to go! A third of the year has passed and you still have twenty-four books to get through. You now realise exactly why some people call it 'shelf-development', as the only thing that seems to be developing here is how impressive your home office looks with this big stack of books.

SLOW AND STEADY

I want now to take you back to Ancient Greece between 620 and 560 BC, where a storyteller called Aesop composed a wide range of fables that can actually help you with modern-day life. One of Aesop's fables was about the tortoise and the hare. You probably already know the story:

The slow and steady tortoise challenges the fast-paced hare to a race. When they set off, the hare very quickly leaves the tortoise behind and, confident that he is going to win, decides to take a nap midway through the race. When he wakes he finds that his slow and steady competitor has won the race.

With everything we do in life, we immediately adopt the strategy of the hare, hitting things at 100 miles per hour with no patience for the realities of the time that it takes to complete things.

I'm going to completely rewind the story now so that you better understand that the best approach to getting more things done in life is to become the tortoise.

Back to January now and you're excited and motivated to up your personal development game this year. You turn to me and ask me to give you a list of all the best books I've ever read. The next day I come back with just one book. Confused, you say: 'I asked you for all the books you have read, not just one!'

I turn to you and say: 'At 8am every morning, when you're having breakfast, I want you to abstain from going on social media, and instead of scrolling through your Instagram feed I want you to read one chapter of this book. Once you have finished the chapter, I want you to post on Facebook the lessons that you have learned from the chapter. You are then to put the book down and not pick it up again until breakfast time tomorrow.'

You do this for an entire month and to your amazement, you have read three books. Not only have you read them, but you really understood them and you now have a deeper awareness of the things you need to do in your life. This is not the only thing you have seen improve in your life. Your Facebook page has grown and people are messaging you, thanking you for all the wisdom that you put out every single day.

You get to the end of the year having consistently read three books a month and finished the year with thirty-six books under your belt. You have a deeper level of understanding of yourself and an increase on your Facebook page of 5,000 followers. What an awesome year it has been!

Reading one chapter per day takes around ten minutes, depending on the chapter. Writing down what you've learned and posting it to others really makes you understand what the information is about, because it hits a different part of your brain.

A great example of this is the PIN for your bank card. Have you ever lent your card to a friend and when they asked you what your PIN is, you struggled to remember it? You're so used to tapping it in that you may have forgotten what the number actually is.

When you tell and teach, you have to develop a much deeper understanding of what you've just absorbed, as you need to really grasp the concept so you can explain it to others.

This, ladies and gents, is my 'One Chapter Per Day' analogy. You can replace this book chapter with a whole host of things in your life — exercise, reading, listening — or working. It all becomes massively effective when you stop looking at the results on a daily and weekly basis and start looking at them in the long term. Two examples below are from my own personal experience and with a client I have worked with online.

LITTLE AND OFTEN

In December 2018 I did a photoshoot and was amazed at the development in my back thickness. I racked my brains trying to figure out how my back had grown so much when I hadn't been paying much attention to making improvements to it. Then I remembered a daily habit that I had been doing since the start of January.

Nearly every morning I'm up by 5.30am and out of the house for a walk down to the beach. There's a pull-up bar on the promenade and a little instruction guide on it for passers-by, with three different levels. If you can do two pull-ups you are a 'beginner', if you can do four pull-ups you're 'intermediate' and if you can do seven pull-ups you are classed as 'advanced'.

It puts a little smile on my face to realise that I can pass this every morning, do seven pull-ups and carry on with my walk in the knowledge that I have become 'advanced' in something so early in the day. Looking back on my year, I had 265 walks, meaning 265 little wins on the pull-up bar doing my seven pull-ups.

If you're not aware of it, when it comes to muscle building there are principles that need to be in place to achieve what's known as 'hypertrophy': an increase in the size of skeletal muscle caused by growth in the size of its component cells. One of the key fundamentals for growth is Volume, which in gym talk is 'Sets × Reps × Weight'.

When we look at my 265 sets of pull-ups for the year, we take the 265 sets, the 7 reps and my weight (90kg bodyweight) and we put it all together to find out the additional volume that has gone through my back over the course of the year. It turns out that the number in kilogrammes is 166,950 – around the same weight as an Airbus A300 aeroplane! This simple daily act of seven pull-ups has put a plane through my back in the course of a year. It's no wonder I've noticed the 'sudden' increase in width.

My second anecdote is that of a client who had committed to get an extra 3,000 steps in each and every day without fail. How he did this was to park his car ten minutes away from his workplace and walk to work. This was easy for him to do consistently as not only was he managing to get his extra steps in, but he managed to listen to every single episode of my podcast, killing two birds with one stone. Super productive!

Now let's imagine that he changed nothing more in his routine than walking an additional 3,000 steps per day; compounded over a year, that's 1,095,000 additional steps. For an average guy walking at an average pace, 10,000 steps will burn around 500kcal, meaning that in a year he will burn an additional 54,000kcal. When we look at 1lb of fat being around 3,500kcal, that means in one year the body would burn 15lb of stored energy.

So, you can see just how much of an impact walking an extra ten minutes a day would have on the body in the space of a year.

TASK

Two of the most important things you must learn when it comes to success in anything are patience and commitment to doing a small amount consistently each day. Imagine what you could achieve in a year.

Here's a list of things you can do that would have huge impacts on your life if you did them every day. Each takes less than ten minutes to do:

> Twenty push-ups a day

> Seven pull-ups a day

> One book chapter per day

> Five minutes' journalling every day

> Messaging appreciation to one person a day

> Learning three new words of a foreign language per day

> Getting better at a skill in ten minutes a day: handstands, throwing, singing

Pick one of these and commit to it for a month. The chances are you will notice an improvement in this space of time, which should help develop the habit and keep it consistent.

Next, you need to do your Meltdown Management Scale and mark each one from 1 to 5.

Chapter 8 scoring	
Health (mental and physical)	
1 – Poor and in desperate need of improvement	
2 – Below average	
3 – Average	
4 – Above average	
5 – Elite	
Wealth (financial and social)	
1 – Struggling with finances and in desperate need of improvement	
2 – Below average	
3 – Average	
4 – Above average	
5 – An abundance of financial and social wealth	
Productivity	
1 – Struggling to get even the smallest task completed each day	
2 – Below average	
3 – Average	
4 – Above average	
5 – A productivity machine	
Connectivity (physical and emotional)	
1 – Barely connect with anyone physically on a daily basis	
2 – Connect with people physically once a week	
3 – Connect with people physically 2–3 times a week	
4 – Connect with people physically and emotionally 3–5 times a week	
5 – Connect with people physically and emotionally every day	
Total	
Average	

RUNNING AVERAGES

Ch. 1	Ch. 2	Ch. 3	Ch. 4	Ch. 5	Ch. 6	Ch. 7	Ch. 8

MORNING AND EVENING ROUTINES

Do you want to know something that you can take that costs absolutely nothing and will help improve your memory, reduce stress, maintain your weight, can actually make you smarter and can also help reduce the risks of depression?

It's sleep.

And do you know the problem with that? When we're stressed and unhappy with our weight, stuck in a rut or feeling depressed, it's probably the last thing on our minds.

I used to be one of those people who said: 'If you got up two hours earlier each day, in a year you would have an entire month extra to get things done.' The reality is that it doesn't really matter how many hours you're awake; it matters what you do with them. And it's hard to be productive and energetic when you're tired.

What relationship does this have with morning routines? Think about it. Mastering what you do when you wake up and mastering what you do before you go to sleep can actually help you have more of it. Routines come down to habits, and habits can be permanent if you see a major benefit from practising them.

Sleep was a huge wake-up call for me in the first year of business before I had my meltdown. It was 1st July and the day we opened my brand-new gym facility for the first time. Because this was an independent gym facility and I wanted to attract other customers who were over the road at another gym, I looked at what time the gym opened and closed.

They opened at 6.30am and closed at 8pm, so naturally I decided to open mine at 5.30am and close it at 9pm. The problem with this was a stark realisation on my first day of opening. The gym is open over fifteen hours per day, seven days per week, meaning we need to staff the place 105 hours per week.

I hadn't really thought about this and had hired only one receptionist for forty hours a week. I thought the best thing for me to do was to do forty hours myself on top of building the business, which meant I was getting there around 5am and closing around 10pm, six to seven days per week.

You've heard of people hustling 100-hour weeks; well, at the time I was clocking in 120-hour weeks and slowly becoming completely exhausted. I remember one morning waking up and it was midday. I had set my alarm for 4am and my body just said no.

This carried on for about five months before I was dragged away for a family holiday. The last thing I wanted at the time was to go on holiday, especially when I was building a business, but deep down, I knew I needed to go. During the holiday I got eight to nine hours of sleep a night and boy did I need it! It was as if my body had a shut-down and was lapping up all the hours it could get. Within three days my brain came alive and ideas started flowing, something that I hadn't felt since I started to build the business. I also realised just what sleep can do for your body.

> *'You'll never change your life until you change something you do daily. The secret of your success is found in your daily routine.'*
> JOHN C MAXWELL

For the past five years, I've had a solid morning routine, but it's only been about eighteen months since I realised the importance of an evening routine. Let's talk about my morning routine first, what you can learn from it and the things that you can do to apply them to your life.

THE MORNING ROUTINE

What you do the minute you wake up is one of the most important things you can think about. In a previous chapter, I spoke about not being able to serve others from an empty cup. Your morning routine is all about preparing and filling that cup with goodness so that you can serve it to others for the rest of the day.

Your morning routine can be five minutes long, fifteen minutes long or even two hours long, like mine. It will all depend on your circumstances, how many kids you have and if you're an early bird or a night owl, as there are benefits and disadvantages to both.

My typical morning routine starts at 5.15am when my alarm goes off. I have my clothes by my side, ready to put on, so that makes getting up much easier. You have to set yourself up to win in the morning, as any excuse when getting started can cause you to hit the snooze button.

The most important thing to think about in a morning routine is to wake up in a proactive state and not a reactive one. If you want to be reactive then wake up, check social media and emails, and it won't be long before you are pouring into someone else's cup. Never do this in the morning; focus on being proactive.

I get up and weigh myself. I usually do this regardless of my goals and I don't really care too much what the scale says, as I'm lucky not to have an emotional attachment to my weight. The practice of weighing myself once again sets me up for the day by telling my brain that this is something I care about.

Social scientist Dan Ariely has studied this practice deeply and has said: 'when we step on the scale in the morning, it has the power to serve as a *reminder* of our commitment to health. Think about it – if you've just stepped on your scale, will you then have oatmeal or a donut for breakfast?'[5]

Next, I get dressed, grab my headphones and listen to a podcast or audiobook. It's safe to say that listening to these has changed my life. Spending an hour most mornings listening to smart people discuss how to get healthier, happier, fitter and stronger has set me up for the life I now live.

The next thing I do is grab my sea bag. This is an ordinary backpack and it contains a tripod, my sea shoes and a towel. I normally sleep in a pair of swim shorts, which acts as a reminder for me to 'get in the sea'.

5 D Ariely (2017) 'When you let a social scientist design for better weight management' [Blog]. http://danariely.com/2017/12/18/when-you-let-a-social-scientist-designs-for-better-weight-management

In previous chapters, I spoke about how cold water has had such an effect on my life, and these cold sea dips have been easy to add to my morning routine. 'Habit hacking' is where you combine a new habit with an existing one, and that is what I have done with my sea dips.

There is just one issue with the sea dips and my morning walk: I really enjoy the walk but the sea dips not as much, especially when the sea is a little choppy or the weather isn't the best. Over the past few months I have found this to be the ultimate conditioning for my productivity, because the last thing I want to do at 6am is jump in an ice-cold sea.

> '*Eat a Live Frog first thing every morning and nothing worse will happen to you the rest of the day.*'
> MARK TWAIN

The sea dips, you see, are my 'Live Frog'. They are something that I do not want to do every day but I do them anyway. If you can condition yourself to do things anyway, regardless of whether you feel like it or not, you can become incredibly successful, especially if these things are done in the morning.

As soon as I am down on the beach, I tend to go live on Facebook. There are two reasons for this: one is the accountability of going in the sea ('people look forward to the live stream and it stops me creating excuses') and the second one is all about content. A lot of what I have spoken about in this book has come from these morning live streams, as my brain is most awake in the mornings.

When I have finished my sea dip, I walk past the pull-up bar and do my daily seven 'think about the plane' pull-ups. Depending on my route, the morning walk takes just over an hour and covers 6,000 steps.

When I get back home in the morning, I have a fifteen- to twenty-minute stretch routine that starts at the feet and works all the way up to my back and neck. This has been a huge addition to my mornings and has enabled me to stay more flexible and less prone to injury. Once finished, I usually read a chapter of a book and prepare my to-do list for the day and my social media. This is more or less what I do seven days per week and my cup is full before I start to serve it to others.

If we break down this routine, you can see what effects it has had on my body and mind. Each morning I am conditioning myself with the sea dips to do things I don't want to do and getting massive benefits mentally from the cold endorphin rush.

I am listening to personal development podcasts, so I am learning something new each day and filling my mind with positivity and optimism.

Each morning I am getting light exercise, from the five-minute swim in the sea to the seven pull-ups on the bar and the 6,000 steps from the walk.

My live stream on Facebook is 'pouring from my cup' and giving value and wisdom to the world, which in turn is therapeutic as I am talking out my thoughts. This, in turn, gets repurposed in podcasts and social media content throughout the week and helps me grow my audience and business.

The reason I talk about the benefits so much is because there are many different practices to achieve them. Use the acronym MESSAGE to remember:

> Meditation – Meditation is anything that helps train attention and awareness and achieves a mentally clear and emotionally calm and stable state.

> Eat the frog – Focus on doing something you don't want to do every single day.

> Set yourself up to win – Make it easy to do your positive habits (lay your clothes out,

charge your phone, download the audiobook for the morning).

> Stretch – A bow that is too tightly strung is
easily broken. Make sure you're loosening
up each day.

> Avoid – Avoid anything that will put you in a
reactive state, such as emails and negativity on social media.

> Give value – Share some good into the world
in the morning and focus on making someone healthier, happier, fitter and stronger;
this will actually help you become healthier,
happier, fitter and stronger.

> Exercise – Exercise is your brain's 'Happi-
ness Medicine'; when you're lean and ac-
tive you feel good about yourself, especially
when you have done it in the morning.

THE EVENING ROUTINE

I am pretty new to evening routines and had never realised the importance of them. Little did I know that my
evening routine was actually more important than my
morning routine, and I'll tell you why. I've never had
much of a problem with my morning routine and getting

up early. Seven years in the Army will do that to you, but one thing I noticed is the difference in me.

For example, my wellbeing and mood during my morning routine were affected when I hadn't had enough sleep. Sure, I would still hit everything, but some of the things were just going through the motions. Speaking to people on the live streams didn't provide as much insight and value to others because I was tired, and when listening to my audiobooks and podcasts, I would feel distracted and unable to listen to the information that was going through my ears. This could all be changed if I got enough sleep and focused on coming up with a strategy to sleep better in the evenings. It starts with where I was going wrong.

In the evenings I would put my laptop down and spend an hour watching some mindless TV to 'relax' after my crazy busy day. The problem was that I didn't relax because I would be on my phone looking at social media. If there was a problem in one of my Facebook groups, I would instantly be responding to the issue and getting it sorted.

If someone had a negative opinion about something online, I'd be first in on the comments to read the arguments and potentially add wood to the fire. This did not work well for my stress levels, or for my business, because arguing on the internet, especially late at night, got no one anywhere. This 'downtime' in front of the TV really wasn't downtime. I could have put anything on the TV because I really wasn't watching it.

In the past, I've been in a relaxed state, checked my phone fifteen minutes before I went to bed and seen there was an argument or issue. I would go into my home office, flip open my laptop and deal with it there and then. The problem with this was that it was now midnight and I should have been fast asleep two hours ago. This issue, which could have been sorted in the morning, had now cost me two hours' sleep.

In previous chapters, I spoke about your energy and discipline being like a battery and as the day goes on you have less and less of it. In order for you to recharge, you need to go to sleep.

When your battery is drained and you go on social media late at night, you lack the discipline to be kind and considerate online. You become emotional and defensive, which is why you should never go on social media after 8pm.

Nothing good ever happens after 8pm on social media.

The first thing that I added to my evening routine was to switch off social media after 8pm. My phone settings are all set to 'do not disturb' and I put my phone in my office.

My next focus for my evening routine is to measure my sleep. Something I tell my audience is that what gets measured gets managed, and if you don't know how much sleep you're getting each night, how can you improve it? There are many different apps out there that can manage your sleep, with new ones being invented every month, so have a look, read the reviews and experiment with a few. Recording my sleep each day has helped me to go to bed earlier because, like a game, I want to get a high score.

My evening routine is also about 'setting myself up to win' for the next day. This involves packing my sea bag the night before, setting out my morning walking clothes and getting changed into my swim shorts before I go to bed. This has made it incredibly easy to get up in the morning, and on days when I really don't want to do a sea dip I say to myself: 'If you didn't want to, then why have you got your swim shorts on?'

The next thing on my evening routine is journalling. I have an app that asks me these eight questions:

> What did you do to improve your health today?

> Did you have fun today and if so, what was it?

> What did you learn today?

> What's the biggest thing you're grateful for today?

> Who do you remember helping today?

> Did you get angry or triggered today? How did you deal with it?

> How have you improved your wealth today?

> What can you do better tomorrow?

Spending five minutes at 7.30pm each evening answering these questions helps me reflect on the day, repeat the good things the next day and try to improve or avoid the negative things the next day too.

The next strategy I had to think about was finding things to do that actually made me want to go to bed early. This came about from reading. Each night I have two books by my bedside. The first is *The Daily Stoic* by Ryan Holiday and Stephen Hanselman.[6] I'm on the second year of reading this book and it takes around three to five minutes a day to

---

6 R Holiday and S Hanselman (2016) *The Daily Stoic: 366 meditations on wisdom, perseverance, and the art of living.* New York: Penguin Random House.

read, which I really look forward to doing. The other book is any current personal development book I have, and I challenge myself to read a chapter before I sleep.

One thing I realised when it came to sleep is that if you struggle to get to sleep, trying to force it doesn't work. The more you force it, the more you resist it. It got me thinking about the opposite effect: when you try to stay awake you end up feeling sleepy, and there are only a few times I remember feeling like this. The first was watching TV after having a skinful of alcohol. I don't think this would be a good idea to add to my evening routine, so let's not focus on that one.

The next one was when I used to allocate thirty minutes in the afternoon to read a paper book. I would get three pages in and struggle to keep awake for some reason. I now realise that it was because a book is non-stimulating compared to a mobile phone. When you read things on electronic devices the light stimulates your brain, and you're getting dopamine hits with the 'Pavlovian pings' of your emails and notifications. With a paper book, you have none of this.

When I challenge myself to read a chapter in bed in the evening, my brain seems to do the opposite. Once again I get three pages in and find myself nodding off to sleep.

Before I am completely wiped out I set my alarm, which plays fifteen minutes of ambient noise. My current favourite is the sound of autumn leaves and for the first thirty seconds, it's quite disrupting. Two minutes in, you start to relax and I have yet to last the full fifteen minutes before I'm sound asleep. There's a lot of research going on at the moment to explain the benefits of ambient noise for sleep and while sleeping, and personally for me it has been effective.

When it comes to an evening routine, remember the acronym SMARTS:

> Switch off social media by 8pm

> Measure and manage your sleep

> Assess the day

> Read a paper book in bed

> Try some ambient sounds

> Set yourself up to win

TASK

It's time to start looking at your own morning and evening routines and seeing where you've been going wrong. For the next week, I want you to write down what you do each morning and what you do before you go to sleep.

Look at my MESSAGE and SMARTS acronyms and try implementing one or two of these actions to see if they have a positive impact on your routines. Once you start to see some benefits the habits will become much easier.

Next, you need to do your Meltdown Management Scale and mark each one from 1 to 5.

Chapter 9 scoring	
Health (mental and physical)	
1 – Poor and in desperate need of improvement	
2 – Below average	
3 – Average	
4 – Above average	
5 – Elite	
Wealth (financial and social)	
1 – Struggling with finances and in desperate need of improvement	
2 – Below average	
3 – Average	
4 – Above average	
5 – An abundance of financial and social wealth	
Productivity	
1 – Struggling to get even the smallest task completed each day	
2 – Below average	
3 – Average	
4 – Above average	
5 – A productivity machine	
Connectivity (physical and emotional)	
1 – Barely connect with anyone physically on a daily basis	
2 – Connect with people physically once a week	
3 – Connect with people physically 2–3 times a week	
4 – Connect with people physically and emotionally 3–5 times a week	
5 – Connect with people physically and emotionally every day	
Total	
Average	

RUNNING AVERAGES

Ch. 1	Ch. 2	Ch. 3	Ch. 4	Ch. 5	Ch. 6	Ch. 7	Ch. 8	Ch. 9

CHAPTER 10

PROTECTING THE ASSET

I went wrong with a lot of things before my meltdown and I was spending a lot of selfless time helping others rather than spending that time with myself and my family. It's easy to keep yourself busy and not address the underlying problems that you have in your life.

> *'Put yourself at the top of your to-do list every single day and the rest will fall into place.'*
> ANON

I am fortunate to be better now at solving my problems and balancing them out by adopting the habits and routines you've been reading about. One of the most important things I want you to do is not to wait until you are broken to be fixed like I did.

You have to protect your most important asset in the world and that is you. In this chapter, I want to break down and summarise exactly how you do this in three of my speciality areas: body, brain and business.

PROTECTING THE ASSET – BODY

To increase the body's strength your focus should be on building your body. There are many benefits to building your body beyond how much better you look naked:

Bone density – This decreases your risk of age-related issues such as osteoporosis (brittle bones) and sarcopenia (muscle loss), which is associated with bone loss (osteopenia).[7] Resting metabolism studies have shown that every pound of untrained muscle uses between five and six calories per day for protein breakdown and synthesis, but every pound of resistance-trained muscle uses about nine calories per day for more extensive protein breakdown and repair processes.[8]

---

7 I Wolff, J Van Croonenborg, H C Kemper, P J Kostense and J W Twisk (1999) 'The Effect of Exercise Training Programs on Bone Mass: A meta-analysis of published controlled trials in pre- and post-menopausal women'. *Osteoporos International*, 9(1), 1–12.

8 B Strasser and W Schobersberger (2011) 'Evidence for Resistance Training as a Treatment Therapy in Obesity'. *Journal of Obesity*, Article ID 482564. http://dx.doi.org/10.1155/2011/482564

There is undeniable evidence of the improvement in the physical and mental quality of your life when you become physically fitter and stronger.

The most important equation to understand is Stress + Rest = Growth:

> Stress — Resistance training, putting tension on the muscle, building up the pressure, finding it harder to breathe, getting uncomfortable.

> Rest — Taking a day off, relaxing the muscles and taking a deload week with your exercise.

> Growth — Stress tears the muscle; rest repairs and grows the muscle. It's vital to tear the muscles in order for them to grow, but they don't just grow in the gym; they also grow when you're resting and repairing.

Stress and rest are the yin and yang of your body and you need adequate amounts of each if you are to become stronger over time.

PROTECTING THE ASSET — BRAIN

You must look at your brain as a muscle in the way that you treat it. If you don't put it through reps and sets it will not become stronger, but if you don't allow it adequate rest it will not grow.

NEUROPLASTICITY

For many years people believed that the connections in our brains were fixed and could not be changed, which led to the belief that you're born with a certain type of brain and you can't do anything to fix it. People, therefore, believed that if they didn't do too well at school it was because they were stupid, and they carried these thoughts throughout their entire lives.

This, of course, is not true.

If you were to look at my school reports or my academic success from when I was younger, the future was not looking too bright for me. I scraped through my GCSEs and only managed to pass one of the two years of the college course I was doing.

A book that opened up my mind to how the brain works was *Peak* by Anders Eriksson and Robert Pool,[9] which spoke about neuroplasticity. Neuroplasticity is the

---

9 A Ericsson and R Peel (2016) *Peak: Secrets from the new science of expertise*. New York: Eamon Dolan/Houghton Mifflin Harcourt.

---

ability of the brain to change continuously throughout an individual's life.

This means that if you put your brain through patterns of learning and understanding with adequate amounts of stress and tension, it will grow. Not only will you become smarter, but you'll be able to deal with a greater work-load and have more capacity, which means you can get a lot more things done in a day.

If I reflect on what I am doing this year compared to what I was doing three years ago, I am actually doing more. My brain now works at a greater capacity and is able to cope much better with the demands that I place on it.

Like a muscle, it's important to understand the equation Stress + Rest = Growth. The thing I missed three years ago was the rest part.

You need to place adequate stress and tension on the brain, by challenging yourself to get better at the things you're passionate about and the things you don't enjoy doing but still must do.

It's taking calculated risks and facing your fears, it's building up confidence in your abilities and constantly seeking new challenges and adventures to continue your brain's growth.

As important as this is to do, you need to adopt the same strategy with the brain's rest and recovery and plan these effectively. This involves:

> Planning times of rest by switching off your emails and social media at the same time each evening

> Taking full-day breaks away from your work and the stresses in your life

> Looking at holidays and mini-breaks away as investments of your time in the knowledge that a fully rested and recovered brain will be able to cope with more stress and tension once it has repaired the 'tears'

If you want bigger biceps in the gym, you don't place stress and tension on them for hours a day, every day, and hope they will grow. You will probably injure yourself and fail in your attempts to make them bigger.

If you want a bigger brain, you don't place stress on it every single day in the hope that you will become successful. You will probably injure yourself like I did in 2016 and take almost two years before it starts growing again.

PROTECTING THE ASSET – BUSINESS

I've learned a lot about business over the years, from running many of my own businesses to helping many people grow their own.

One important thing to realise is that a business is there to solve problems. The more problems you are solving for your customers, the more they talk about you and the more you continue to grow.

One important thing to focus on is that a business isn't just you. If like me, you have a personal brand as a business, this may lead you to think that no one else can do the work except you. This is totally incorrect. A personal brand is just that: a brand.

To me, a brand is a signature in your business that reminds people of its quality regardless of who is delivering the product. If you work hard on this brand, no matter who is delivering your product it will be delivered in the same way. This is one of the biggest things for you to grow in your business, as it allows you to work with more people and to scale up.

Unlike your body and brain, you can place continual stress and tension on your business and watch it grow without the need for rest and recovery. Why is this? Because most of the time there is more than one of you in your business, so when one is resting and recovering the other can step in and place the stress and tension on the business. If you're your business's biggest asset, you need to focus on growing the team around you so that you can always play at your highest level.

Apply the Eisenhower Decision Matrix to your business and working life. Do things that you need to do, delegate things you don't need to do and, most importantly, don't forget to delete the things you don't need to do.

TASK

My task for you is to look at your body, brain and business and ask yourself if you have the right balance for each one.

With your body, are you exercising it regularly and giving yourself plenty of time to rest and recover? Are you challenging yourself mentally and allocating time off and time away?

Are you playing at full capacity in your business and allowing others to hold the fort while you recharge your batteries?

When was the last time you really rested? Took a holiday or had a few days off? You need to look at these days as investments of your time, not distractions. Stress + Rest = Growth, so make sure you are planning out your rest days so that you can continue to grow.

Next, you need to do your Meltdown Management Scale and mark each one from 1 to 5.

Chapter 10 scoring

Health (mental and physical)

1 – Poor and in desperate need of improvement	
2 – Below average	
3 – Average	
4 – Above average	
5 – Elite	

Wealth (financial and social)

1 – Struggling with finances and in desperate need of improvement	
2 – Below average	
3 – Average	
4 – Above average	
5 – An abundance of financial and social wealth	

Productivity

1 – Struggling to get even the smallest task completed each day	
2 – Below average	
3 – Average	
4 – Above average	
5 – A productivity machine	

Connectivity (physical and emotional)

1 – Barely connect with anyone physically on a daily basis	
2 – Connect with people physically once a week	
3 – Connect with people physically 2–3 times a week	
4 – Connect with people physically and emotionally 3–5 times a week	
5 – Connect with people physically and emotionally every day	
Total	
Average	

RUNNING AVERAGES

Ch. 1	Ch. 2	Ch. 3	Ch. 4	Ch. 5	Ch. 6	Ch. 7	Ch. 8	Ch. 9	Ch. 10

CHECK YOURSELF BEFORE YOU WRECK YOURSELF

Insanity is doing the same things over and over again and expecting a different result.

When I looked back in my career of becoming a personal trainer after being made redundant, I realised that the first time I had ever written down my thoughts and feelings was when I was completely lost and didn't know what I wanted to do. In the past, I had not considered just how much I enjoyed

'I will keep constant watch over myself and – most usefully – will put each day up for review. For this is what makes us evil – that none of us looks back upon our own lives. We reflect upon only that which we are about to do. And yet our plans for the future descend from the past.'
MARCUS AURELIUS

helping people with their nutrition, training and mindset goals, and I was plodding along being miserable in a well-paid but incredibly unrewarding job.

Ask yourself this question: when was the last time you wrote down your current satisfaction levels with what you're doing in life?

Many people will not address their problems because they are not willing to face them. If we are unhappy about our weight, we will do everything to avoid situations where the issue becomes highlighted, such as standing on the scale, trying on new clothes and even possibly going on theme park rides and taking flights abroad. If we're struggling with money, we try our best to avoid looking at our bank account because it makes us unhappy, much like the scale.

The trouble with doing this is that it doesn't solve the problem. It merely masks the problem and moves it on to another day, potentially becoming a bigger problem later when you go deeper and deeper into debt or become heavier and heavier on the scale.

It's vital that we check ourselves before we wreck ourselves, and this is where daily, weekly and monthly reviews come into our lives, but how you manage each one is different. I'm going to look at the difference between them so that you can better understand the reasons for them.

DAILY REVIEWS

It's important to spend at least five minutes each day checking in with yourself to see if you're on the right path. The best way to look at this is to imagine an aeroplane flying to its destination. Along the way, it needs to correct its course, based on the weather and the winds, and this is why we do a daily review.

The daily review is not about reaching our destination; it's merely checking to see if we are sticking to the correct habits each day so that we get there. I created the Meltdown Management Scale because it gives you daily feedback on the things you need to improve the next day.

If you haven't prioritised your health today, make it more of a priority to exercise and eat healthily tomorrow. If you haven't focused on improving your connectivity today, make sure you catch up with a friend and be social tomorrow. When we don't check in with ourselves each day, it's not long before we go way off track from where we want to get to, and it's much harder to course-correct as now we have to go to the opposite end of the extremes to balance it out.

Your daily review is about ticking boxes and being aware of your habits and routines, not seeing big improvements.

WEEKLY REVIEWS

Your weekly reviews will build up a better picture of your habits and routines than your daily reviews will. What we want to do is to take an average of the overall score from each day. Having this way of thinking with any habit you have is so important, as it allows you to play the game much better.

Let's say you allocated 2,000kcal per day to lose weight and on Wednesday you consumed 2,500kcal. If we were to judge our progress based on a daily review, we would feel like a failure, and this kind of thinking could lead us to failure.

Let's say though that we took those 2,000kcal and multiplied them by seven to give us 14,000 kcal for the week. We are playing a bigger game now, and although you failed to stay under your target for the day you can still win the game by the end of the week by course-correcting slightly and reducing calories for the rest of the week.

What a 'perfect' week would look like:

Monday – 2,000kcal

Tuesday – 2,000kcal

Wednesday – 2,000kcal

Thursday – 2,000kcal

Friday – 2,000kcal

Saturday – 2,000kcal

Sunday – 2,000kcal

Total = 14,000kcal

Average day = 2,000kcal

What actually happened and how we can fix it:

Monday – 2,000kcal

Tuesday – 2,000kcal

Wednesday – 2,500kcal

Thursday – 1,900kcal

Friday – 1,800kcal

Saturday – 1,900kcal

Sunday – 1,900kcal

Total = 14,000kcal

Average day = 2,000kcal

Your weekly reviews should be an average of each day of the week, but your daily reviews will give you feedback on how to course-correct through the week.

Our focus each day is on awareness of the things that need to be improved and the most important ones to prioritise, so that we can improve the weekly average score. Let's see how this would look based on the Meltdown Management Health Scale:

Health

Monday – 3

Tuesday – 3

Wednesday – 4

Thursday – 4

Friday – 2

Saturday – 3

Sunday – 4

Average score = 3.2

Overall, you have an average level of health.

MONTHLY REVIEWS

Monthly reviews are one of the most important things to focus on so that you can understand whether you are making true progress or not. A month of measuring your progress will give you enough data to really determine if you are moving the needle forward in your health, wealth, productivity and connectivity.

With the monthly reviews, you will be taking the average scores from each week and finding out your average for the month. Let's see how this would look on the Meltdown Management Health Scale:

Week 1 — 3.2

Week 2 — 3.4

Week 3 — 3.8

Week 4 — 3.4

Monthly average = 3.4

You are between average and above average with your level of physical and mental health.

By now you might be thinking that this system is too complex, but it isn't. It goes back to my 'one chapter per day' analogy, because all you are really doing is spending five minutes each day doing the Meltdown Management Scale. The rest of the work is just taking the data and working out the averages to review what is currently working in your health, wealth, productivity and connectivity and what needs more work.

TASK

Commit to doing the Meltdown Management Scale for a month. Each day, spend five minutes putting a number by your health, wealth, productivity and connectivity. To do this successfully, set a reminder to do it at the end of each day and make it 'non-negotiable' to get it completed.

Each week, take an average of the scores and jot it down (the days added together and divided by seven). Reflect on the days that were good, the days that were bad and the course corrections you applied to improve them.

By the end of the month, you will have a clearer picture of what your focus needs to be. For me, it was my connectivity. My score was so low that it made me realise that something needed to drastically change in my life if I was to see some improvements, and I made a conscious effort to improve my habits in these areas.

Finally, make sure you do your Meltdown Management Scale for today and mark each one from 1 to 5.

Chapter 11 scoring	
Health (mental and physical)	
1 – Poor and in desperate need of improvement	
2 – Below average	
3 – Average	
4 – Above average	
5 – Elite	
Wealth (financial and social)	
1 – Struggling with finances and in desperate need of improvement	
2 – Below average	
3 – Average	
4 – Above average	
5 – An abundance of financial and social wealth	
Productivity	
1 – Struggling to get even the smallest task completed each day	
2 – Below average	
3 – Average	
4 – Above average	
5 – A productivity machine	
Connectivity (physical and emotional)	
1 – Barely connect with anyone physically on a daily basis	
2 – Connect with people physically once a week	
3 – Connect with people physically 2–3 times a week	
4 – Connect with people physically and emotionally 3–5 times a week	
5 – Connect with people physically and emotionally every day	
Total	
Average	

RUNNING AVERAGES

Ch. 1	Ch. 2	Ch. 3	Ch. 4	Ch. 5	Ch. 6	Ch. 7	Ch. 8	Ch. 9	Ch. 10	Ch. 11

THE HAPPINESS HYPOTHESIS

Looking back at my life and its ups and downs, I've never really searched for happiness directly; it's kind of found me along the way when I have felt that some-

> *'Happiness is an inside job.'*
> WILLIAM ARTHUR WARD

thing wasn't right and needed to change. Over the years I've come up with my own hypothesis on nine different focuses that, if you get them right, will lead you to a better life:

1. Health
2. Action
3. Persistence
4. Passion
5. Integrity
6. Novelty

7. Empathy
8. Selfishness
9. Selflessness

This chapter is dedicated to exploring each of these so that you can better understand how to apply them in your life. Trust me when I say that if you wake up every day with these as your focus, you will start feeling more content, fulfilled and happy.

HEALTH

So many people think that the epitome of health is having a six-pack and bulging muscles when that couldn't be further from the truth. There is certainly a correlation between someone who looks fit and their happiness, because to achieve the level of physique that it takes to stand out from the crowd, you need a lot of discipline in your life.

Coming from a competitor background, I have seen first-hand some incredibly happy fitness competitors, yet I have also seen some unhappy and depressed ones too. As with everything we have spoken about in this book, you have to be extremely selfish to become a world-class fitness competitor, which means 'tipping the scale' for long periods of time. This can be as much of a disadvantage as an advantage, and having an incredible-looking physique doesn't always mean you are happy with it.

When we look at health, we aren't just looking at physical health; we are looking at mental health too. Mental health is a growing concern, and one of the most shocking statistics I have seen in the past year is that eighty-four men take their own lives every week in the UK.[10] When their families are asked about it, they often didn't know anything about it and found that the individual kept everything from them. When it comes to physical health, a lot of our lifestyle factors and illnesses can be outwardly visible to others, but when it comes to mental health, this is often not the case.

It's important to treat both physical and mental health with the same level of importance and attention if happiness is what you are looking to achieve.

ACTION

I was reading an incredible book by John C Maxwell called *The 15 Invaluable Laws of Growth* and he said

---

10 www.ons.gov.uk/peoplepopulationandcommunity/birthsdeaths andmarriages/deaths/bulletins/suicidesintheunitedkingdom/ 2018registrations#suicides-in-the-uk

something that stuck with me about people and personal growth.[11] He broke people down into three categories:

> People who don't know what they want to do

> People who know what they want to do and don't do it

> People who know what they want to do and do it

When it comes to the first two types, action is one of their biggest issues and lack of it is stopping them from succeeding. Much of this inaction and procrastination is due to a large number of things, including:

> Fear of failure

> Lack of meaning

> Self-doubt

> Perfectionism

> Laziness

> Distraction

---

11 J C Maxwell (2012) *The 15 Invaluable Laws of Growth: Live them and reach your potential*. New York: Center Street.

People are concerned that if they take action on their dreams and it doesn't work out, they will become a laughing stock. This is certainly not true, as other people have so much of their own lives caught up with their own goals and dreams that they fail to have any time to judge yours.

People wait for the perfect time to launch something, hoping that there is going to be a perfect gap in their lives to absorb all the information and make a real go of it. This is never going to be a reality, and as Reid Hoffman, the founder of LinkedIn once said, 'If you are not embarrassed by the first version of your product, you've launched too late.'

The final one I will speak about is 'distraction', as it's one of the biggest issues at the moment. Technology is growing at an exponential rate and we now have the world at our fingertips. The electronic devices in our pockets have the ability to make us skinny, rich and happy, yet a lot of the time they are making us fat, lazy and skint. You have to build discipline with your devices and know when to use them to absorb good quality information that is going to make you healthier, happier, fitter and stronger and when they are going to cause you to waste time and become distracted.

PERSISTENCE

This is defined as 'a firm continuance in a course of action in spite of difficulty or opposition.'

I was asked the other day what I thought the best advice was to give to a new personal trainer and I said: 'To never give up.'

Success has never been an overnight thing for me. I have been in my industry for over seven years now and seen many people come and go. There are also many people who have achieved what I have in half the amount of time. I get asked how I built a large social media following and my answer has always been 'showing up every day and delivering value'.

I created my Instagram page in April 2012 and have shown up every day consistently. It's only been in the past couple of years that things have really started to take off, and I'm glad that it has only just started to advance as it has given me plenty of time to prepare and get ready for it.

During your life and career, you're going to have massive highs and massive lows, and the key to succeeding through all of it is showing up every day and pressing forward.

PASSION

I have spoken in depth about passion over the past few years and to a certain extent I disagree with the quote 'If you love what you do, you will never work a day in your life'.

To yourself, you won't feel like you're working, as you love what you do and spend a crazy number of hours doing it. But to your family and friends it is work, and I have shared with you first-hand how this has been an issue for me and for many other people.

To be happy you *must* do something that you love to do, but really focus on exactly what that is, as the answer isn't always to build your own business doing it. Being incredibly happy and fulfilled building someone else's business makes a lot more sense than being miserable and tired building your own.

Write down the things you are passionate about and a list of things that you are better at than most people. See if there is a common factor between the two and if there's a possibility that you could turn it into a product or service to help others.

INTEGRITY

There was a film many years ago called *The Truman Show* starring Jim Carrey. It was a fascinating film which showed Jim's character Truman as the unsuspecting star of The Truman Show, a reality television programme broadcast live around the clock worldwide. Everyone knew it was a television programme, except him.

To me, this is a mental model that can help you maintain and better understand integrity. If you were Truman in this TV show, are your actions and habits in line with the things you are telling others and leading you on the path to success? It's what you do when no one is looking that has a real impact on your life, and 'what you practise in private you are rewarded for in public' (Tony Robbins).

Integrity is about doing the right thing, even if at the time it's easier to ignore it. It's reminding yourself of your personal values when it comes to people and progress. Integrity is one of the biggest assets you can have in building your body, brain and business.

NOVELTY

To me, novelty is going against the grain of what is normal so that you stand out from the crowd, and sometimes it's doing the opposite of what you need to do to progress. To many people, when they think of the word 'business' they imagine suits, ties and briefcases, which is why you will never see me looking like this.

When it comes to my business and marketing, I like to make things look fun and enjoyable, which makes it stand out from the crowd. Novelty sparks curiosity in others and gives them permission to have fun themselves.

Always seek to find your own way of doing things. As I've mentioned before, there are very few fundamentals but there are an incredible number of methods to achieve them. Add the 'fun' into fundamental with your own habits and routines and those of your customers and clients, and you will start to feel more content and happy.

EMPATHY

When I left the Army back in 2009, empathy was something that I struggled with. I had just spent seven years in military service working around highly disciplined individuals who were told what to do and just got on with doing it. There wasn't much procrastination and there weren't many people who were lazy or complained, and when I left I was surprised when someone told me that they were going to do something and didn't manage to do it.

It didn't take me long to realise just how lucky I was that I joined the military at such a young age. From seventeen years of age, I had a sergeant yelling over my shoulder telling me what to wear, how to walk and where I needed to be, and as long as I paid attention to these things and took action, my life was pretty easy.

If I had not joined the Army at such a young age I really don't know where I would be now, as at that time I needed someone to yell at me and tell me what to do. These days I am my own drill sergeant and, thanks to my own daily practices, I have managed to succeed in this quite well.

My development in my knowledge and application of nutrition, training and mindset has given me the tools to help others 'level up'. I can quite confidently say that I play these things at a very high level and it's now my mission to help others with theirs.

To me, empathy is listening to others and trying my best to understand their problems, regardless of how they are expressing themselves. If they are being angry towards me and trying to bring me down, this is a sign that they need help, not that I should go up against them and try to bring them down.

Empathy is knowing what level I'm on and trying my best to figure out what level the person that I am speaking to is currently on. If I have already completed that level, then I will be showing that person how I completed that part of the game, and at the same time, when I figure out that the person is playing at a higher level than I am, I will ask questions and sit and listen to find out how to solve this level of the game.

SELFISHNESS

We have spoken in depth about selfishness, and to achieve happiness you need to make sure you are 'filling up your cup' every single day. These selfish practices are reading, learning, exercising and allocating personal time to get healthier, happier, fitter and stronger so that you can best serve others. You are the most important person in the world and you help more people when you are at your best.

SELFLESSNESS

You are rewarded in this world based on the value that you give to it, and your selfless actions towards others will push you forward in your pursuit of happiness. Make sure you are waking up each and every day in a proactive mindset thinking 'what can I give the world today?', instead of waking up in a reactive state of mind thinking 'what has the world got in store today?'.

As already touched on in this book, my favourite quote is 'Give and forget, receive and remember'. Your focus needs to be on giving people gifts every single day without expecting anything in return. Owing to reciprocity, it's only a matter of time before people start to pay it back in full.

TASK

Happiness can be developed in a number of ways but it is not a destination that you arrive at. It is based on daily practices and as you build the habits they become easier to do and you start to smile more.

Health – Are you in good health and are you taking small daily steps to maintain and improve it?

Action – Are you taking action on the things that you know will push the needle forward?

Persistence – Are you giving up at the first sign of failure or using it as feedback for improvement?

Passion – Do you love what you do and do it every day?

Integrity – If people were watching the TV show of your life, would you be proud of how you act each day?

Novelty – Are you having fun and taking the time each day to do something that makes you laugh?

Empathy – Are you getting angry and being triggered by people or are you learning to build up empathy and understanding for others' reactions and responses?

Selfishness – Are you making steps each day to fill up your own cup so you can best serve others?

Selflessness – Are you giving people gifts of your time and knowledge each day without expecting anything in return?

Next, you need to do your Meltdown Management Scale and mark each one from 1 to 5.

Chapter 12 scoring

Health (mental and physical)

1 – Poor and in desperate need of improvement	
2 – Below average	
3 – Average	
4 – Above average	
5 – Elite	

Wealth (financial and social)

1 – Struggling with finances and in desperate need of improvement	
2 – Below average	
3 – Average	
4 – Above average	
5 – An abundance of financial and social wealth	

Productivity

1 – Struggling to get even the smallest task completed each day	
2 – Below average	
3 – Average	
4 – Above average	
5 – A productivity machine	

Connectivity (physical and emotional)

1 – Barely connect with anyone physically on a daily basis	
2 – Connect with people physically once a week	
3 – Connect with people physically 2–3 times a week	
4 – Connect with people physically and emotionally 3–5 times a week	
5 – Connect with people physically and emotionally every day	
Total	
Average	

RUNNING AVERAGES

Ch. 1	Ch. 2	Ch. 3	Ch. 4	Ch. 5	Ch. 6	Ch. 7	Ch. 8	Ch. 9	Ch. 10	Ch. 11	Ch. 12

CONCLUSION

I'm coming to the end of one of the busiest years in my life for my body, brain and business and have finished this year happy, content and fulfilled. In hindsight, 2016 was the best thing that ever happened to me. Without the meltdown, I would not be the person I am today.

People only get better with experience if they are willing to learn and understand the lessons that are given to them through the bad times in their lives.

Now, my routines are balanced and I have a strong understanding of how to balance the scales each side to even them out. This has come from three years of deep self-assessment work, and using the tools that I have shared in these chapters.

My business is booming, my family life is awesome and I really hope that adopting just one or two of these tools will have the same impact on your life too.

I want to finish this book by giving you two concepts to take away when it comes to using the tools in this book: digging for gold and planting the seeds.

DIGGING FOR GOLD

You have all the tools you need to succeed and, as I say to my clients, 'I can give you the tools and tell you exactly where to dig, but it's you that has to dig.'

Use the tools I have given you and move in the right direction with your progress. No matter how sharp the tools are, it's still going to take persistent work for many years before you unlock the gold; and when you do, it's time to get your map out again and look for the next hidden treasure.

PLANTING THE SEEDS

Each day you need to plant the seeds for success. The thing about planting seeds is that if you stare at them every day, they never look as if they are growing. If you plant enough seeds in the knowledge that they will grow, don't focus on the results — just focus on doing the work every single day.

> '*Sometimes the seeds you sow take a while to grow, be patient as you always see a harvest.*'
> JOHN C MAXWELL

Some seeds start to sprout and grow after a few months, but to see the real growth in anything you may have to wait a number of years.

Focus on your 'one chapter per day' and commit to doing the work every single day in the knowledge that over time it will produce the success that you seek. Your hardships can always turn into happiness if you allow them to do so.

I genuinely hope you have got a lot from this book and I would love to hear from you on social media. The best place to reach me is Instagram: @jayalderton. If you post anything be sure to use the hashtag #MELTDOWN as I will be following this hashtag to keep up with everyone.

To access the bonus gifts from this book head on over to www.meltdownbook.co.uk and register for some free goodies.

ACKNOWLEDGEMENTS

My first acknowledgement goes to my wife Anna. She is a true superstar in my life who has been with me through thick and thin and through every up and down. I could not do what I do without her by my side, encouraging me and being my rock in this journey called life.

To my daughter Elyza and son Archer, I do this for you and I can't wait for you to read my books as you grow older in the hope that they help you become understanding towards others, compassionate towards worthy causes and focused on pursuing your dreams. I will always be there for you and no matter what you do with your lives, you will always have my full support.

My next acknowledgement is to my team Jason and Dawid. You guys have been an incredible force in my business over the past two years and I couldn't do this without your support and friendship, so thank you.

To my close friends Dan Meredith, Phil Graham and Michael Banna, I want to thank you for your support and your friendship over these past few years. You have helped me through some tough times, supported me on my journey, and your critical thinking and focus on personal development have kept me inspired and motivated. You guys are only ever a phone call away, something I value and appreciate daily.

And my final shout-out goes to you reading this book and everyone who follows my journey on social media. You hold me accountable for my actions and invest your time in my content and work. You have allowed me to live a life I never thought possible, and for that I will always be there for you to keep you focused and motivated through my content and work. You guys rock!

THE AUTHOR

Jamie Alderton is a best-selling author, athlete and entrepreneur who coaches personal trainers and small businesses with regard to their bodies, brains and businesses.

After leaving the British Army in December 2009, Jamie's passion for self-development and self-improvement led him on a rollercoaster journey through physical and mental transformation.

In 2010 Jamie was British Natural Bodybuilding Champion and proceeded to win his Pro Card as European Muscle Model Champion in 2012, competing on the world stage in 2014.

Since 2012 Jamie has transformed the lives of over 8,000 clients through his products and programmes and continues to grow a successful personal brand and business.

In a constant quest to push his physical and mental boundaries, Jamie has raised tens of thousands of pounds for charity, achieving some insane endurance records:

In 2016 he pushed a 140kg sled for twenty-four hours, breaking a world record.

In 2017 he ran *backwards* for twenty-four hours, covering 109km and raising over £21k for a local children's charity.

In 2019 Jamie set a new Guinness World Record by Box Jumping the Height of Mount Everest, and has raised over £25,000 for a local children's charity.

Jamie does these things so that he can delve into the depths of his body and brain to dig out the gold and share it with his audience to help them on their journeys to becoming healthier, happier, fitter and stronger.

To find out more about Jamie, you can reach him through his socials:

- www.instagram.com/jayalderton
- www.twitter.com/jayalderton
- www.facebook.com/jayaldertonofficial